RV Having Fun Yet?

Ray Parker

RV Having Fun Yet?

Foreword by
Art Linkletter

Oldfield Publishing Company
Durango, Colorado

Published by
Oldfield Publishing Company
425 Iron King Road, Durango, CO 81301

Printed and bound in the United States of America.

Library of Congress Catalog Number: 94-65905

ISBN 0-9640924-0-9 12.95

*

Oldfield Publishing books are available at special discounts for bulk purchases for sales promotions, premiums, fund-raisng or educational use. Special editions or book excerpts can also be arranged. For details contact the publisher.

Illustrations by Gary McAllister, Phoenix, AZ
Cover design by Linda Geer, Durango Illustration and Design
Typography by Roy Paul, Cortez, CO

Portions of material in this book first appeared in *MotorHome* and *Trailer Life* magazines, published by TL Enterprises, Camarillo, CA.

FIRST EDITION

To my wife, best friend and favorite companion, Ethel. Her loving nature, kindly wisdom and unfailing good humor have made our marriage the joy of my life.

Acknowledgements

Behind the scenes of every book, there are people who first encouraged it, and helped bring it into the world. It was fun-loving Bob Livingston, then editor of *Motor-Home Magazine,* who first suggested that I write a monthly humor column for him about our adventures and misadventures on the road. Barbara Leonard as editor of *Trailer Life* was most helpful, publishing some of my earliest articles about life aboard an RV.

I'm also grateful for the advice of Gaylord Maxwell, one of America's leading authorities on RV travel and the author of that excellent book, "Fulltiming," and of Beverly Edwards, editor at-large for *Highways,* the Good Sam Club's publication.

Special thanks goes to Rena Copperman of TL Enterprises Book Division, and to publishing consultant Marilyn Ross of About Books, Inc., for their excellent suggestions. Good friends Jeff and Linda Mannix read the original manuscript and offered several ideas, as did Susan Streeper and Ann and Howard Guss, who also helped me through the intricacies of getting into print.

And finally, a tip of the RV cap to Art Linkletter, a wonderful entertainer and master ad-libber who gave me my first big break in comedy as head writer for "Art Linkletter's House Party" on CBS-TV.

Contents

Foreword

Years ago I became famous for spontaneous humor and it's high time that I acknowledge my thanks to Ray Parker for writing some of my best ad-libs. His sense of the absurd was unfailing because his mind interprets everything he sees on the bias. While everyone else watches life as it actually happens, Ray looks at it through the prism of the outrageous and absurd.

Interviewing kids from 4 to 10 years of age was easy after working with Ray because he never grew up and lost the sense of play. His most unexpected replies were always delivered with the serious attitude of a mortician. Put this kind of a guy in an RV with an adoring wife and a dog and everything that happens takes on a glorious glow of fun. His most exasperating adventures somehow turn out to be what happens to a fat man in a fun house.

You'll chuckle over this book if you've never even stepped into an RV. If you're an old hand at cross-country traveling, you'll howl at the chapter on RV Park restrooms. My own favorite is the story of how Ray dragged his wife out of a comfortable, settled home and, kicking and screaming, into the life of a peripatetic gypsy.

Don't ever quit, Ray. The world is in great need of laughter.

ART LINKLETTER

Introduction

By Bob Livingston
Consulting Editor
  Trailer Life and *MotorHome* magazines
Technical Editor
  Highway Magazine.

It's not difficult to understand why so many folks dream about changing the status quo in their lives. Many of us are locked into stressful lifestyles with little hope for change. We work, we raise the kids, pay the bills, complete the honey-do's and continue the same daily cycle.

But eventually, after the grey hairs start showing up (or the hair goes away altogether), some thing wonderful happens and the dreams hopefully become reality.

We get to retire.

In today's active world, most retirees want some type of leisure activity that will keep the old blood flowing, like buying a motorhome and traveling this great land of ours. But if your mate enjoys staying at home, you might get a reaction that will make the cold war seem like child's play.

Suddenly, routine practical matters involving the house, the kids and grandkids and finances become almost insurmountable obstacles to a travelling lifestyle. But buying an RV was exactly what Ray Parker was determined to do, convincing his lovely wife that they could live happily within the confines of a 280-square-foot home that was, indeed, very mobile.

Parker commemorated his victory on the matrimonial battlefield by penning, "How I Dragged My Wife Kicking and Screaming into a Motorhome." I was the editor of MotorHome magazine at the time and had the privilege of publishing this piece.

While Parker has a long list of credentials as a writer of very funny stuff, the real life situations he encountered as a novice motorhome traveler provide hilarious realism to fellow RV enthusiasts who have lived through similar experiences. Parker's story of his first trip in a motorhome, "The First Time," really activated the funny bones of our readers.

We all recognize that not every motorhome adventure will be funny. There are times when simple events like wrong turns can become near disasters. But laughing is a natural response to funny situations, whether they involve getting lost in impossible places, comical campground embarrassments or the refrigerator door opening on a mountainous road, sending eggs into orbit and spattering everywhere. And so, "Backroads," a monthly column authored by Parker and reserved for the last page of the magazine, was born, along with a long-time relationship with a writer who has an uncanny ability to find the brighter side of life.

Not only is Parker a funny guy, he's spent lots of time out there among other RVers. His experiences with his motorhome and contacts with other people who shared his lifestyle provided a natural environment to collect material for this book. Parker is a master at taking the simple actions and daily activities of RV people and converting them into comedy routines. He even pokes fun at himself. And I can guarantee that you're gonna laugh!

Without a doubt, Ray Parker's collection of experiences will make "RV Having Fun Yet" a must read for any RV enthusiast. As you peruse the pages of this highly original book, keep in mind that everything here actually happened. Sit back, and enjoy!

How I Dragged My Wife Kicking and Screaming Into a Motorhome

WHEN I DECIDED IT WAS finally time to kiss the old job goodbye and have fun traveling the country, I had to face the awkward fact that my wife was perfectly happy with our life at home.

Ethel loved our house in the suburbs of Los Angeles with all its familiar furnishings and possessions. Our grown children lived nearby, where she could see them often. So did all our lifelong friends who were always ready for a cozy lunch or a walk in the foothills.

But I had grown weary of battling Southern California's crazy-making freeways to get to work. I felt like Sisyphus, that hard-luck character in Greek mythology who was doomed for eternity to roll a huge boulder up a hill each day, only to have it roll down again.

I yearned to escape from relentless office deadlines, decisions and jangling phones. I'd had enough of doing my daily soft-shoe on the slippery slopes of office politics.

Besides, I felt I deserved a chance to relax and take it easier. After all, I had earned several campaign stars in the trenches of child-raising, as well as a parental purple heart for surviving that memorable siege when all six of our kids were teenagers at the same time.

I day-dreamed of taking off a big chunk of time to enjoy what advertising copywriters in their thirties call "The Golden Years." But I knew this would never happen unless I was prepared to yank my wife up by her roots and drag her away, kicking and screaming.

I couldn't just say, "I'm thinking of quitting work and traveling around the USA. How about it?" Persuading her to agree would take the same gentle wariness of a male spider courting a black widow. Not that my wife would do me in, necessarily, but she does know her own mind. If I came on too abruptly, I knew she'd put her foot down, and my neck would be under it.

To set the right mood, I suggested we meet for dinner at her favorite Italian restaurant in West Los Angeles. Then, as she sipped a glass of white burgundy, I gently tested the marital waters.

"Honey, we haven't gone on a trip in a long time. Wouldn't it be fun for the two of us to get away for a while?

She eyed me a moment and said, "Please get up off your knees. You know I hate groveling."

"I'm not groveling," I said. "It's my freeway sciatica kicking up again."

She seemed relieved to hear that I wasn't abasing myself, but merely in pain.

"What do you have in mind?" she asked. "A long weekend? San Francisco, maybe?"

I hesitated. "More time than that."

"Oh, you mean a vacation."

"Well, not exactly, but kind of, in a longer sense, you might say."

"Stop mumbling, Ray! How can I understand what you're saying when you keep chewing your napkin like that?"

"Well, what it is, you see, is —"

"The point, dear, the point."

"I'd like to, ah, quit work and take a year off to travel."

Her eyes became the size of our salad plates. "You can't be serious. A whole year? Why?"

I do think I explained it rather well, considering that she kept staring at me like a doctor thinking about putting me away where I wouldn't hurt myself. Finally she said, "I sympathize with how you feel, dear, but we must be practical. We just can't afford to go gallivanting around the country."

"Sure we can," I said, "if we sell the house."

"Sell the house? The place we've lived for twenty years and raised our children?"

"Or rent it," I said. "We'd have some income for travel expenses that way."

"Ha!," she said. "What about bills like car payments?"

"No problem," I said. "We'll sell the cars."

"Sell the cars?"

"We wouldn't need them. Not after we buy a motorhome."

Her voice escalated into a shriek: "*A what???*"

If I'd been that amorous spider I mentioned earlier, I would have revved up all eight legs and run for cover.

Fortunately, the waiter rescued me by returning with menus. I ordered her more wine, and retreated behind the pasta list until she muttered something about fettucini, which meant it was safe to come out.

That's how the Great RV Debate got under way. It lasted, on and off, for several months as I kept devising new ways to win her over.

I tried the "life-can-be-beautiful" approach:

"Just picture the two of us, free of cares, heading down life's highway together. No mortgage, no daily commuting, no alarm clocks."

"Uh huh. And no home, no job, no income . . ."

I tried philosophy:

"Honey, did you ever stop to think that we modern Americans are possessed by our possessions?"

"And did you ever stop to think," she retorted, "that if you don't keep working, all our possessions will be repossessed?"

I tried melodrama:

"I can't work forever. Would you rather see me work myself into an early grave, and leave you a prosperous widow?"

She seemed to brighten a bit. But all she said was, "Don't you think it might help if you talked all this over with Carol's husband?"

"The psychiatrist?" I was indignant. "Are you suggesting that my elevator no longer reaches the top floor? You think I'm a quart low, with only one oar in the water and a wheel in the sand — is that it?"

"No," she said, "but he's a good friend, he's about your age, and it would be interesting to hear his opinion on making a big life change like this."

I had to admit this was a sensible suggestion. Actually the talk with Sidney the Shrink went quite pleasantly, for Sidney sometimes has long stretches of lucidity. In fact, he was quite sympathetic. "I'd like to see the country in an RV myself," he said. But when I reported this to Ethel, she said, "That's wonderful, dear. Sidney can go with you."

The debate might have gone on forever, if our car hadn't mysteriously quit running, right in front of an RV dealer's showroom.

While we waited for the Auto Club service truck, I persuaded her to come inside with me and look around. When she saw what a modern RV looks like, she was impressed despite herself.

"I was expecting a cracker box on wheels," she admitted as we were shown through the interior of a 30-foot dream machine. It had paneled oak cabinetry, two TV sets, a stereo system, the latest convection microwave oven, a countertop blender and many other dire necessities.

Meanwhile the Auto Club man had discovered a rare malfunction in our car. The ignition key had somehow switched itself off. As we drove away, I noticed the beginnings of a change in Ethel's attitude toward recreational vehicles. She no longer made those odd frothing noises when the subject came up.

During the next several weeks, we cruised around from one dealer to another, getting familiar with various makes and styles of motorhomes. I decided that a 22-footer would meet our needs nicely, without breaking the piggy bank. But Ethel had other ideas.

"If I'm going to live in one of these," she announced, "I'm going to pick it out." Finally she decided on a fancy 35-footer that had all the creature comforts imaginable, with extra oaken closets and a queen size island bed. It was a solemn yet joyful moment as I realized my dream was about to come true. Tears began misting in my eyes, and Ethel was touched. I didn't have the heart to tell her that I was crying about the price tag.

The First Time

SELLING MY WIFE ON THE idea of an RV lifestyle was no more difficult, say, than persuading her to tour Tibet on a skateboard. The real challenge came after we purchased our motor home. She refused to ride in it.

I think she was suffering from *Primophobia* — fear of the first time. It's a common condition, often felt by young lovers who are getting serious. She was being the female who worries about possible consequences down the road, while I, the pleasure-seeking male, could hardly wait to get started.

Actually, Ethel had a point. I'd never driven anything bigger than a station wagon, yet now I was about to take the wheel of a 35-foot vehicle, an entire home on wheels that looked big enough to have its own ZIP code.

"I'll follow along behind in our pickup with the dogs," she said. (That was a smooth touch about our two dogs; she wasn't risking *their* necks, either.)

I protested. "What's there to worry about? All kinds of people have driven these things all over the world."

She eyed me thoughtfully. "You haven't."

From then on, I knew I'd have to earn my wings as an RV pilot, while she flew tail-end Charlie in the pickup.

Since I'd had no RV experience, the salesman babied me through explanations of fresh water tanks, gray water tanks, black-water tanks, the generator and electrical systems, instrument panels, and much more, including gizmos like hydraulic levelers and a fancy TV camera mounted in back that watches one's rear end.

As the dizzying details kept piling up, I began wondering if there wasn't some way I could just join the wife and dogs in the pickup, while some graduate of M.I.T. drove the RV.

Eventually, after the dealer loaded me down with a wheelbarrow or so of instruction booklets, I decided I'd manage somehow. So off we went to our first destination, the corner gas station.

I was vaguely aware that it takes a lot of gas for motorhomes to have a decent cruising range. But I hardly expected that first fueling session to up and suck that station dry. As the dials on the pump kept spinning, my grip on the nozzle went numb. I was getting pumper's cramp in both hands, and still hadn't finished filling the first tank. Finally, when both tanks had guzzled nearly 100 gallons altogether, I gave the happy attendant my charge card. I kept my eyes shut while he ran the total, because there are some things it is best not to know. I was consoled somewhat by the thought that I could now travel across entire States before needing to refuel.

As I pulled out of the gas station in Los Angeles and picked up speed, hoping to reach Las Vegas, Nevada by sundown, my ears were assailed with all kinds of alarming crashes and bangs. Had we blown a tire? Had the transmission fallen into the street? Had I run over a moving van without noticing?

I looked back down the aisle and saw drawers of canned goods hurling themselves onto the floor, closet doors slamming wildly, and dishes clattering like a quake in a china shop. Obviously we hadn't packed in proper RV fashion, so now I had a rolling shivaree on my hands.

After a hasty stop to stuff everything back more or less where it belonged, I rolled along for hours without further problems until we reached the long desert upgrade near the Nevada border. It was a sizzling late summer afternoon, with temperatures well over 100 degrees, and both of our motorhome air-conditioners were working their little fans off.

As we gained altitude, we began passing a number of panting vehicles of all kinds that were pulled over with their hoods up, trying to cool off. Soon my own engine began surging, slowing and surging again, like a frog with hiccups, threatening to come down with vapor lock. I started wondering if a pickup could tow an RV. Yet somehow the engine never quit entirely, and I surged onward and upward.

The sun had set before we reached the motor-home park in Las Vegas. Ethel and the dogs — a white male standard poodle named Charles and a sweet female Doberman who answers occasionally to Lena — came warily aboard the RV for the night.

"The dogs are thirsty, and so am I," said Ethel. I turned on the tap, but nothing happened. Then I remembered I hadn't filled the fresh water tank, wherever it was. And even if I had found and filled it, I couldn't remember what the salesman said about

operating the water pump anyhow, wherever that was.

Seeing my blank look, Ethel suggested I connect a hose to the park's faucet. That I could do. Soon we had water, then power, and even television — all the comforts of home. As the warm glow of TV filled the motorhome, like an electronic hearth, I felt pretty good about our first day on the road.

A Dicey Time
in Vegas

WE SPENT A WEEK IN LAS Vegas, and I cannot say it was all hijinks, jackpots and fun in the sun. Everything was hot except the dice. The sizzling sunshine was wilting thermometers, reaching 108 degrees. We got our exercise sprinting from one shade tree to another.

As for our surging engine, the local dealer looked at the undercarriage and said, "Good news. I can see exactly what's wrong."

"Great," I said. "How soon can you fix it?"

"That's the bad news," he said. "Too many rigs ahead of you."

Fortunately, we found a shop where welders could do what we needed — to fabricate a heat shield to protect the fuel line from the exhaust's heat build-up.

With the heat shield installed, the engine surge departed. So did we, for Tonopah, en route to the cool pines of Lake Tahoe. As we rolled out of the Vegas RV park, people came running out to wave at us.

"Now that's what I call friendly," I said to Ethel.

"They're not waving goodbye," she said, "They're pointing at our roof!" I slammed on the brakes, realizing I'd forgotten to crank down our TV antenna.

That kind of beginner's boo-boo no longer happens to me, because I now use a pilot-style checklist that I developed the hard way. It includes such urgent forget-me-nots as the water hose that I once left connected while driving off, and the main power cord that also followed us down the road like a lonesome umbilical.

A key item on our personal list involves putting the lid on the dog kibble bucket. If you think that lidding kibble is a trifling matter, you should try scooping up 20 pounds of the stuff after the bucket has overturned and made a skating rink of your rig.

I would like to report that Ethel now trusted me at the wheel, and was happy to be at my side as we traveled through the shimmering heat toward Tonopah.

But the truth is, she drove the pickup again. Her excuse was that the motorhome engine would run cooler if it didn't have to haul the truck along behind. But she knew, and I knew, and she knew I knew, that she still thought I'd be better at driving a team of yaks than a multi ton motorhome.

The journey to Tonopah went smoothly, without a hint of overheating. But when we arrived, we made the mistake of asking a local teenager where to go for dinner. Never, never do that.

Our obliging adolescent steered us to a genuine Western watering hole where horny-handed silver miners in denims, and ranch hands with gaudy tooled leather boots and ten gallon hats were lined up along an ancient mahogany bar, happily lapping up the suds. It was a scene from an old John Wayne movie, and it made me want to mosey up and join 'em.

But Ethel had food on her mind, so we took a table and ordered burgers and fries. The burgers were passable, I suppose, if you have a taste for incinerated doilies, but the French fries were as well oiled as the bar crowd. We were so hungry we tried to eat the fries anyhow, but they kept squirting off the plate. I figure I could have stuffed those fries into our crankcase and made it to the next town, easy.

After an overnight stay in a pleasantly wooded little RV park, we were ready to head on into Tahoe country. Again I invited Ethel to ride with me, and, to my astonishment, she said she would. Evidently the cautious, by-the-book driving I'd done for the last several hundred miles, all without sideswiping a single state trooper car, had made an impression.

The dogs, however, remained unconvinced. As I fired up the engine, they exchanged panicky looks. Their "home" was starting to roll down the highway. The dobie dived under Ethel's feet on the passenger's side and cowered under the dashboard, while the poodle scampered amidships and skidded under the dinette. Then each peered out with reproachful eyes, with much the same look Ethel had when I suggested buying a motorhome in the first place. After an hour or so of riding, however, the dogs recovered their spirits somewhat, becoming accustomed to the idea of a traveling house.

With Ethel now at my side as we rumbled up the long, steep grade to Lake Tahoe, I was beginning to feel pretty salty, like an experienced highway highballer. You'd have thought I had just been nominated for the Teamster Hall of Fame.

I had no way of knowing that a treacherous comeuppance was lying in ambush down the road at a little bridge in Auburn, California — but that's getting ahead of the story.

After the scorching desert, the South Lake Tahoe campground was an oasis of coolness. We turned off the air-conditioners and breathed in that delicious, pine-scented mountain air. The dogs had a great time romping through the woods. And as Ethel and I strolled amid the big trees, we could see that this was what RVing was all about.

Not that we didn't have problems, even in this piney paradise. As I tried to shoehorn the RV backward between trees into my parking space that first night, a bystander suggested I go back around and head straight in. I ended up picking my way down an almost invisible path fit only for skinny chipmunks.

The next challenge came after dinner as Ethel climbed into bed, and slid right back out again, like a dollar rejected by a money-changing machine. "The bed is slanting downhill," she said. "Can't you fix that?" This meant I would have to burrow into that mountain of manuals in the back closet, to figure out how to use the hydraulic gadgets for leveling the coach.

"I'll get to it first thing in the morning," I promised.

"You'd better fix it now," she replied, "unless you're batty enough to sleep while hanging by your toes."

After digging up the right manual, I spent the next hour or so turning various knobs that cranked the motorhome up, down and sideways until it was level enough for a night's sleep.

Next morning, I had to face setting up our hi-tech awning. Even its brochure was awesome, listing no less than 27 steps involved in raising and lowering the thing. After studying all the instructions, I knew what I must do: Get help!

That awning was like a 25-foot Rubik's cube to me, so I was quite surprised when a kindly neighbor casually coaxed it into shape in no time. Then he admitted that he'd spent his whole life in the hardware business.

Holy Smoking Radials!

BUNGEE JUMPING IS A sissy sport compared to being a rookie RVer at the wheel of a nine-ton rig as it hurtles down the notorious Donner Pass grade.

I thought I knew enough about momentum in a heavy vehicle to watch our acceleration, but it was truly frightening to be practically standing on the brakes while the gears whined louder and louder. I had visions of hurtling toward doom at ninety miles an hour, praying for a ramp marked "Runaway Trucks."

It felt like that big drop on a roller coaster, except that at an amusement park, you know you'll probably live to ride something else.

By the time we reached bottom, our brakes smelled like a barbecue in a tire factory. Holy smoking radials! Later I learned that more experienced RVers make a practice of stopping to cool their brakes on long downgrades.

I suppose my guard was down after putting all that white-knuckle driving behind me, for I was quite relaxed as we approached Auburn, California, in the Mother Lode country. We planned to stay at the Dry Creek Inn, a bed-and-breakfast run by the wife of an old combat buddy in the Eighth Air Force.

Our innkeeper friend, Lois Maggenti, had told me over the phone that the only access to her place was a one-lane wooden bridge over the creek. She assured me it would be no problem. "Trucks use it all the time," she said. (None of those trucks were 35 feet long, we discovered later.)

As I reached the address, I stared in disbelief at the creek bridge itself, which barely qualified as a one-laner. I had serious qualms about committing 35 feet of motorhome to what looked like a rickety old pile of boards.

But now traffic was building behind me. Horns honked, and somehow I found myself inching forward and turning onto the bridge to get out of the way. Onward I went, the big rig rumbling heavily over the wooden ties. So far, so good . . .

Suddenly I heard a "crrrunch" of telescoping wood and metal. Ethel, who had just arrived behind me, yelled, "Stop! Back up!" My right rear bumper, which I couldn't see, had caught on a railing and was ripping the bridge apart like a giant crowbar.

A crowd gathered to watch as though we were some great ship that had run aground. I tried to stay calm, inching backward until the bumper finally snapped free of the railing. Then, with a volunteer guidance crew big enough to launch a space shuttle, I babied the big machine on across the bridge.

But that wasn't the end of it. Now I had to squeak around a sharp left turn, backing up and pulling forward several times until I could move on down the one-lane road to the inn.

Upon reaching the inn, we faced the worst predicament of all. How would we ever get out again?

Backing up was out of the question. The road, cut into a hillside, was far too narrow for turning around. Should we call in a cargo helicopter to lift us out, thereby becoming the first airborne RVers? Like Scarlett O'Hara, we decided to think about that tomorrow.

Up a Creek

IF THERE'S ONE THING worse than being up a creek without a paddle, it's being up a creek in a 35-foot motorhome, with no way to back out. As predicaments go, this one ranks right up there with tripping over a bee hive at a nudist camp.

Even an apprentice RVer like myself could see that there was hardly room to turn a golf cart around on the Dry Creek Inn's access road, a narrow one-laner between creek and hillside. Backing out looked equally impossible, because of the road's 90-degree turn at the wooden creek bridge.

But we had to get back onto the main road eventually, or else convert our RV into a creekside diner. It was too big for a planter.

Actually we did have a few other notions, such as trying to float it back across the creek like an ark, or letting the bank come repossess it, just to see the look on the bank guy's face when he saw where it was.

"Maybe you could sell it for scrap," said Lois, our Dry Creek hostess. "If you drive out the way you drove in, you're going to wreck it anyhow."

I spent the evening hours quietly mulling the problem, interrupted only by Ethel's occasional shrieks of "Stop thrashing around and go to sleep!"

Sure enough, I had an idea the very next morning while taking a shower. (Archimedes did his best thinking in the tub, remember? Good clean thoughts they were, too.)

"Eureka!" I cried, wrapping myself in a towel and loping down the hall to tell Ethel: "We'll clear off their back yard and make enough room to *turn the motorhome around!*"

To tell the truth, I wasn't too sure this could work. I'd be stuck in close quarters again, this time between a stand of backyard trees and the hillside. I'd have only inches to jockey back and forth in, but it was worth a try. At worst, I'd end up with a tall, thin motorhome. But first we'd have to remove a massive pile of heavy timbers and railroad ties, and clear away a thick patch of brush. All this would take yard tools, a strong back and hours of hard labor. Since I lacked the first two, and had spent my life avoiding the third, I asked Lois if we could hire someone to clear our launching pad.

She called in a shrewd young neighbor who agreed to clear out her yard in exchange for my wallet. Late that afternoon, both yard and wallet were empty, and all was ready for an attempt at a turnaround.

While another gallery gathered to watch, I revved the engine and drove slowly up onto the newly cleared plateau. As I'd feared, there were only a few inches of space for maneuvering. But with the young neighbor standing behind the rig, yelling instructions to help me use every inch, I rocked the big machine back and forth like a baby buggy, gaining a few degrees of angle at a time. Finally, all 35 feet of motorhome was turned completely around. A cheer went up from the cheap seats. We were on our way! Or were we?

Still ahead lay the most worrisome challenge, that tight right turn onto the little wooden bridge. Squeezing the RV around that corner would be like cramming an elephant into a phone booth.

Ethel got out, either to help or avoid drowning. Then I shifted into low and sent the big rig rumbling forward.

It didn't help any to see the bridge rails still sagging crazily after I scrunched them on the way in. I had offered to repair them, but our hostess had decided to wait until I was safely out of her neighborhood.

I tried to encourage myself, remembering what Sidney the Shrink had to say about situations like this. "Whenever you're so worried about a problem that you can't think of anything else," said Sidney, "ask yourself what's the worst that can happen. Often you'll see that the worst isn't really a disaster at all, but something you can deal with and take in your stride."

Sidney was right. I leaned out the driver's window to Ethel, who was now minding the front bumper so it wouldn't smash the bridge posts into kindling again, and said, "Well, honey, what's the worst that can happen?"

"You could wreck the bridge and dump our RV into the creek," she said.

Thus reassured, I swung the machine out toward the far side of the bridge. Then I began the same maneuver that worked in the back yard — rocking back and forth to bring the rear end in line with the bridge itself. Meanwhile the bystanders shouted directions, encouragements and a scattering of rather insensitive remarks whenever the front wheels wandered over the edge.

Many sweat beads later, I finally rolled the rig into the clear on the bridge's wooden planks. The gallery cheered. "You see?" I said to Ethel. "It was a piece of cake." Rare indeed are such moments of elation in a man's life.

"Congratulations," she said. "Now let's see if we can pry your fingers off the steering wheel."

The Write Stuff

ONE OF THE MOST
enjoyable assignments I ever had was putting the
"Dear Abby" radio show together for that remarkable
lady when she was on CBS. I was credited as the
writer, but all I really had to do was assemble material
for broadcast that Abigail Van Buren had written herself. Now, if Abby will forgive the poaching on her
territory, here are some motorhome letters:

Dear Ray,

*As somebody whose husband is thinking of buying
an RV for year-round use, I have two questions:*

*(1) How do RV's keep their water hoses from
freezing in cold weather?*

*(2) Do you think a trip with just the two of us in
an RV would make my husband more romantic?*

Signed,

"Wondering."

Dear Wondering,

You can buy electrical wraparound tape to warm
up motorhome plumbing, but that won't work on
your husband. However, an RV vacation may be just
what's needed. Plan a trip way out into the boon-
docks, where the only evening entertainment is you,
and let nature take its course.

Dear Ray,

My wife's been after me for years to watch my diet, but I still love burgers and fries, and I hate that dumb rabbit food she likes to fix. So I'm overweight — who isn't? Now she's really on my case and says I've turned into a big fat turkey. What should I do?
Signed,
Tom

Dear Tom,

Just be glad your wife cares enough to worry about your health, you turkey. Either get serious about shaping up, or make yourself scarce next Thanksgiving.

Dear Ray,

Now that my husband is retired, he's decided to take up cooking. At first I thought it was a great idea. After raising three kids and fixing a zillion meals, who needs to cook?

But now I'm having second thoughts, because our motorhome galley is constantly piled high with pots and pans that the great chef expects me to wash.

Not only that, he puts wine into everything, including the soup. And by the time he finishes nipping at the cooking sherry, he can hardly find the dining table with both hands.

What do you do about a husband who thinks he's Julia Child?
Signed,
"Fed Up"

Dear Fed,

First, I'd ask the great chef to clean up as he goes

along, before he's too schnockered on sherry to tell a pot from a pint. He should also agree to do his share of the dishes when the gourmet feast is over. After all, you're the lady of the house, not the scullery maid.

Other than that, I see no great harm in a food lover like your husband playing Julia Child, unless he starts wearing dresses.

> *Dear Ray,*
>
> *My new boyfriend just bought a motorhome and wants me to take a weekend trip with him to try it out. Should I?*
> *Signed,*
> *"Tempted"*

Dear Tempted,

It all depends on how far you want to go.

> *Dear Ray,*
>
> *What can I do with a husband who ruins our travels with his snoring? I tried sleeping up front in the fold-out couch while he sleeps in back, but I can still hear him snoring away like a buzz saw all night long. Any advice?*
> *Signed,*
> *"All Tuckered out"*

Dear Tuckered,

First, see if you can roll him over. That often stops the music. If it doesn't, try having him sleep in the fold-out couch. Then, as soon as he starts snoring, fold the couch on him. He may not stop snoring, but at least you won't hear him.

Dear Ray,

All I keep reading about these days is safe sex. What's your advice for interested RVers?
Signed,
"Just Curious"

Dear Curious,

There's no such thing as safe sex in an RV unless you pull over and park.

Dear Ray,

After full-timing on the road for nearly a year, our motorhome is starting to look like a Salvation Army warehouse because my husband never throws anything away. He insists on saving worthless stuff like old fishing pants and worn-out boots that he never wears, and broken reels and other gadgets that he never fixes. When I object, he says, "Those things may come in handy."
Signed,
"Pack Rat's Wife"

Dear Wife,

Just wait until he's gone fishing or whatever, and then dump all that junk in the trash. With a little luck, you'll both be hundreds of miles down the road before he notices anything's missing.

Dear Ray,

I'm writing about the scandalous behavior of a young woman in our RV park. Every night this

shameless bimbo gets undressed with her shades up, and every man in camp knows it. Would you prefer charges?
Signed,
"Shocked"

Dear Shocked,
No, I'd prefer to see all the evidence myself.

Tiny Dog Park

OUR TROUBLES BEGAN when we pulled into the RV park, and saw the sign at the entrance: "Small Dogs Only. Max. Height 18 In."

Thinking of our standard poodle, my wife turned to me and asked, "How tall is Charles?"

"About 2 feet, give or take a couple of inches," I said.

She frowned. "He's too big."

"Maybe we can teach him to crouch," I said. "He wouldn't look so tall if he walked on his knuckles."

(For anyone doubting that Charles could *learn* to crouch, I offer this example of his versatility: He is trained to do his business on command. We stop at a likely place, command him to "Go doors," and he goes instantly into scanning mode, seeking a suitable bush. From command to execution seldom takes over sixty seconds.)

When I asked the pleasant young woman at the office about whether the park actually enforced the canine height limit, she was reassuring. "I've seen a few bigger dogs here, and nobody seems to mind as long as they don't cause any problems," she said.

"Then I guess we're okay with our sweet and well-behaved poodle," said Ethel.

Not!

After several days of chauffeuring Charles to the doggie powder room area, my wife was emboldened to take him for a romp in the adjoining county park. But as they neared the exit, with Charles trotting on leash beside Ethel's bike, a woman with a jail matron's voice shouted, "That dog doesn't belong here!"

Ethel turned to see a lady leaning out of a car window, looking grimmer than a tax assessor.

"No dogs are allowed to *walk* in this park," the woman said. "Pick up that dog!'"

Pick up *that* dog? Charles is no teacup poodle. He weighs at least 50 pounds. And Ethel is no weight lifter. She just stood there in disbelief while the woman grilled her, as if Ethel had just been caught smuggling kilos of coke from Columbia.

"How did you get in here?" the woman demanded.

"Why do you ask?" countered Ethel, who was reluctant to implicate the desk clerk that we'd asked about the sign.

"I'm the manager here," the woman said. "If you want to stay, that big dog must go."

Ethel tried to explain that other RV parks had complimented us on Charles' model behavior, but the woman was adamant.

"No dogs over 18 inches," she repeated. "Didn't you read the sign?"

She ordered Ethel to report to the office immediately, and drove off.

But instead of following her, Ethel hurried Charles back to our RV, hid her bicycle and drew the shades like a fugitive, to gain time until I returned and we could talk it over.

My first reaction was one of principle, to protest how Ethel had been treated, and then check out. But this place was a garden of Eden on a scenic bay beside a beautiful park, and we were lucky to have a space there at the height of the snowbird season. What good are principles when you're having fun?

Besides, some old friends from Chicago had just flown 2,000 miles to join us here. Leaving just didn't make sense.

"Maybe we can work out a compromise," I said.

"If you met the lady, you wouldn't say that," huffed Ethel.

I began to wonder if we could ride this out by keeping a low profile for a while, until the manager could cool down and forget us.

It was a good thing we hadn't also brought along our Doberman, another 50-pounder who was back in Los Angeles at the moment, visiting her mother.

"Did that woman get your name or space number?" I asked. "No."

"Then she has no idea who or where we are, or even how long we'll be here," I said. "This is a big park. She might never find us if you don't go back to the office."

On the other hand, we wondered how happy Charles could be as a four-footed felon, trapped for a month in our RV, never daring to lift his snout above window level. And what about when he had to go doors? If we ran practice drills, I might be able to dash outside and heave him into the pickup in as little as five seconds flat. But once we reached the dog run, he could still be spotted by some bigoted Chihuahua fancier who'd snitch to the matron.

Meanwhile, the manager had evidently grown weary of waiting for Ethel to turn herself in, and was prowling the park to find her.

"Here she comes," said Ethel, peeking out the drapes as her nemesis cruised by in her car, coldly eyeing every RV. Moments later, other members of what appeared to be a park posse — employees in little blue electric carts — came whirring by.

I glanced down at Charles. How could anyone not want *this* dog in their park? Charles is a gentleman to the tip of his toe pads, a yuppie puppy who has never disgraced his breed in any way.

That night, we talked about possibly giving Charlie up for a month or so, if we could find a place where he could be happy. A young poodle fancier, Lisa Gonzales, volunteered that he'd be welcome in her San Diego apartment. We knew this would please Charles, since he is a ladies' man anyhow.

Next morning we gathered up Charles' kibble and dishware, his security blanket and Froggy, his favorite toy, and drove him to Lisa's place. Charles frisked around the apartment, enjoying himself. But when we said goodbye, he gazed at us with those soulful eyes, obviously at a loss to understand why his family was leaving without him.

We enjoyed our stay in Tiny Dog Park, but life just wasn't the same until we were reunited with both our canine traveling companions. Then we set forth, Four Musketeers, all for one and one for all, spirits bright and tails held high.

Rx for RVers

TRAVELING IN AN RV IS A healthy life, with plenty of opportunities for fresh air, sunshine and exercise. However, there are certain hazards and ailments you should know about that are peculiar to life on the road.

Since only those medical people who own RVs are really aware of these maladies, I feel a duty to alert you to certain ills to be wary of in your travels.

Rocky Mountain Palsy: A condition affecting boondockers in mountainous areas who wake up to discover that the place they backed into the night before is on the edge of a 1,000-foot cliff. The best way to avoid those morning shakes is to take one simple precaution when you park in the dark: Before going to bed, get out of your RV and check the back tires. If they are in mid-air, you have backed up too far.

Doorsucker's Disease: Intense fear of being blown off the road as an 18-wheeler rumbles by at 70 miles per hour, nearly sucking the doors off your RV. This disease was named for that notorious common carrier, Barney Doorsucker, a pioneer road menace who ultimately perished from Lead-Foot Poisoning.

Tripper's Mania: The uncontrollable urge to drive at least 100 miles more than you did yesterday. This compulsion often develops into the more serious

Boondocker's Depression, brought on by the inability to find a decent RV park after midnight.

Tailgatosis: A form of claustrophobia induced by discovering that an oil tanker booming along at breakneck speed is climbing up your back bumper. (Although tailgating is not included in the Trucker's Manual of Courtesy, it is quite popular among a macho minority of gearjammers.) The best treatment for Tailgatosis is to pull over and let the roadhog squeal on by.

Turnoff Tachycardia: An excessively rapid heartbeat brought on in crowded metropolitan areas by the need to find your turnoff in heavy traffic on a multi-level interchange while traveling at freeway speeds. Many Turnoff Tachycardiacs also start hyperventilating, and expressing their anxieties in bleepish language.

Divehicularitis: A knotting of the driver's innards at the sight of a steep downgrade. Sometimes accompanied by *Donner's Dementia,* an overpowering feeling of panic and imminent doom, as first experienced by early RVers hurtling down the Donner Pass grade. Treatment consists in pulling over at regular intervals to cool your overheated emotions as well as the brakes.

Parker's Myopia: A mysterious inability to see trees, power boxes or hose pipes lurking behind your motorhome while attempting to back into a parking space. Most commonly afflicts new RV owners. This condition usually clears up rapidly after a few crunches into fixed objects, especially if a repair bill is involved.

Propain: Intense gas pains brought on by finding

you have run out of propane to cook breakfast or heat your motorhome on a frosty morning. Symptoms include chills, hunger pangs, and a tendency to feel rather fuelish. Since it's so painful, this condition tends not to repeat itself.

Packer's Amnesia: The total inability to remember where you have put anything. Most often affects overworked mothers of large families who are exhausted after packing enough clothes and supplies for a parachute regiment, in less time than it takes a 4-year-old to get her jammies on. Victims are often seized by fits of rummaging, and cannot stop until they have turned the entire RV upside down.

Teletonia: A trance-like state that afflicts both soap-opera and sports addicts after several straight days in front of an RV TV. Teletoniacs gradually lose the ability to move a muscle except to eat snacks, and do not recognize as food anything that is not advertised in commercials.

If left unattended, these pitiful people eventually forget how to talk. The treatment of choice is to gently lead or carry the victim outdoors in hopes of arousal by fresh air and exercise. If this does not revive the victim, a tubal block must be performed. That is, the victim must be blocked from viewing the tube until beginning to show signs of recovery, such as recognizing their mates or children.

Petacosis: A form of chronic insomnia brought on by a pet that keeps waking you up in the middle of the night to be taken outside. While there is no known cure for this steadily debilitating disease, it often helps to snore very loudly to create the impression that you're sound asleep, so that your mate will get up instead.

Watt's Disease: This malady strikes at night without warning in older parks with limited power facilities. Everything electrical suddenly goes pfffft because the park can't cope with the combined drawdown from a rig's TV, VCR, air-conditioner, microwave oven, toaster, blender, travel iron and hair dryer.

The victim's blood pressure rises rapidly and he becomes manic, dashing about outside in the dark to find the circuit breakers while shrieking in pain and rage as he stumbles over power cords, water hoses and tree roots. Those who have suffered a severe attack of Watt's Disease often go into *Amporexia,* the overwhelming fear of plugging in more than one amperage-hungry appliance at a time.

Flusher's Block: A condition often precipitated by tossing non-degradables into the RV's toilet. When acute, it causes Plumber's Fit, a foaming tantrum thrown by whoever has to fix it, as well as *Hopper's Disease,* wherein a victim deprived too long of bathroom facilities begins hopping about and screaming, "Hurry up!"

Antenna Envy: This disease of the electronic age is now showing up in remote areas where ordinary TV antennas can't pull in a picture. Antenna Envy is an irresistible compulsion to run out and spend several hundred dollars on a satellite dish, after seeing that your dish-equipped neighbor is watching *The Academy Awards* when you can't even get old reruns of *Bowling for Dollars.*

Wedding-Go-Round

I THINK THERE'S A stowaway aboard our RV. It's the ghost of Murphy, who wrote those famous Laws: 1) Nothing is as easy as it seems; and 2) If anything can go wrong, it probably will.

Murphy showed himself soon after we were invited to a formal church wedding in La Jolla, California. The groom's mother was Ethel's dearest friend. Could we come? We were camped just a few hours away in the mountains northeast of San Diego, so why not? What we failed to realize, in the glow of the moment, was that we had nothing aboard to wear for anything dressier than a Cub Scout cookout. Ethel's finery was stored back home. So was my wedding and funeral suit, a blue pinstripe so conservative you could bury a banker in it.

We could imagine how a wedding reporter might describe us if we showed up in our RV outfits:

"Mrs. Parker was stunning in her off-the-shoulder T-shirt, with coordinated white gym socks, magenta jogging shoes by Nike and jeans by Levi. Her husband was quietly distinguished in faded khaki shorts, a boldly striped sports shirt emblazoned with an alligator, and a bright red billed cap advertising a brand of fishing line."

No, it just wouldn't do.

And even if we did find some decent clothes, we wouldn't have a place to put them on, because our motorhome was due to go into the shop in San Diego on the morning of the wedding.

Nor was clothing the only problem. Our traveling companions — Charles the Standard Poodle and Lena the Doberman — would have to ride to the wedding with us in the front seat of the little pickup truck we tow about. And after several dusty weeks in the mountains, Charles urgently needed a bath, as did the truck. But we really wanted to go, so we came down off the mountain to shop for clothes and a wedding present.

We returned to camp that night to face the next crisis: wrestling Charles into the rig's shower, our on-the-road version of a poodle parlor. What a disaster that was. Charles' wriggly, thrashing body took up the entire shower space, so Ethel and I crouched outside, trapped between shower and commode, rinsing him with the shower hose while dousing him with doggy shampoo. After an endless round of soapings and rinsings, enough dirt cascaded off him to fill a window planter.

Meanwhile, despite Ethel's urgings to "Hold still, Charles!" he kept shaking himself and drenching us with soapsuds. It was steamy, exhausting work. Then we had to towel him down, comb him out, and finish him off with a hair dryer, which took forever. Finally we showered our own thoroughly dogified bodies, and staggered to bed.

The situation started getting out of hand in the early hours of the morning, when a surprise tropical

storm sneaked up from Mexico and let loose a Niag-
ara of rain, making a swamp of our campsite. As I
stumbled out into the downpour at dawn to take the
protesting dogs to the bushes, my shoes sank squishily
into adobe gunk. The campsite looked as if it had
taken a direct hit from a mud bomb. Our Astroturf-
covered parking spot had enough water on it to grow
rice.

When I returned with the dogs, Ethel moaned at
the sight of a newly muddied Charles, who appeared
to be wearing knee-length brown socks. Ethel
dragged him back to the shower for another round of
wrestling while I sloshed around outside, disconnect-
ing everything so we could drive off.

The wedding was now only a few hours away.
We gulped down some coffee and toast, then loaded
the damp dogs, our clean clothes and the wedding
gift into the truck, hoping to keep all the cleans away
from the dirties.

After we dropped off the motorhome at the shop,
I drove the truck toward La Jolla while Ethel tried to
keep Charles from chewing the ribbon off the wedding package. We still needed a place to change
clothes, and Ethel had an inspiration. "Let's stop at
Tiny Dog Park." (That's her name for the place
where Charles was evicted for being over 18 inches
tall.)

Since the notorious Charles was still canina non
grata at Tiny Dog, we drove in past the park office,
pretending to be registered guests. Ethel slipped into
the washroom while I took the truck to the wash
rack. By the time the truck and I were presentable,
Ethel emerged in her new clothes. I hardly recog-

nized her without those magenta jogging shoes.

The sun was shining as we reached the church with only minutes to spare, parking around back where the dogs could be left in the shade.

But now we had a new problem — keeping straight not only who was who among the wedding guests, but who was whose. For this was a typical California ceremony, with enough remarrieds and stepthises and thats to drive a genealogist to drink.

We were close friends of the groom's mother and stepfather, but we had known the groom's mother and real father back when they were married, as well as the stepfather and his previous wife when they were married. Ethel and the groom's mom had been teachers together at a co-op nursery school when the groom-to-be was a toddler.

By now, however, the groom's mother was long since divorced from his father, and remarried to the father of two of the bridesmaids, who were thus step-sisters of the groom and his two brothers, who were raised by the stepfather.

The groom's father also had remarried, so we were meeting his new wife for the first time. The stepfather's first wife, mother of the bridesmaids, had also remarried, so we met her new mate as well. And all this marital merry-go-rounding was just on the groom's side of the aisle. I never dared inquire about the bride's family, for fear someone would tell me.

Nevertheless, the ceremony went off perfectly. The bride was a beaming brunette who had made her own beautiful seed-pearl wedding dress. The brides-maids were also California beauties and the groom and his ushers were handsome lads in morning coats.

The bride had a smile that lit up the church, and she kissed the groom so enthusiastically that the congregation grinned in delight. At the reception that followed, all the parents, stepparents, new mates and ex-mates blended in together and had a wonderful time.

Then we drove off in our shiny truck with our shiny dogs, smiling at our shiny selves. We hadn't looked this dressed up since we started traveling. And the experience was worth it, Murphy or no Murphy. It was such fun that I'd recommend that all RVers attend a wedding occasionally — every twelve months or 10,000 miles, whichever comes first.

Gorillas of the Road

WHERE DOES AN 800-pound gorilla sleep? . . . Anywhere he wants.

It's a kid's joke, based on the idea that anything as big as a gorilla can do whatever it likes.

I was reminded of that gorilla recently when a gargantuan truck and trailer blasted past our motorhome at 70-plus miles an hour, creating a battering ram of air pressure that literally shoved us aside. It was scary, and it could have been dangerous.

Time was when long-haul truckers were known as skilled, safe and sensible drivers. They were professionals, and proud of it. But the trucker's image has been suffering lately, especially since deregulation made a roadside diner hash of the industry's rates and practices.

Professional truckers now must share the road with a lesser breed of scofflaws and economic cutthroats who drive unsafe rigs at unsafe speeds, in unfair competition with everyone else.

I'll tip my RVer's cap any time to the good-guy truckers who are on the road in every kind of weather, day and night, so that you and I can have fresh food and reasonably priced goods at our local stores.

They're easy company on the highway, flicking

their lights before they move on by, or letting us know when it's safe to pass them. They're knights of the road who help motorists in trouble. And when they are done driving for a living, many become RVers themselves.

But what about the bad guys? They're the ones in my rogues' gallery:

Rod Hottley is a grown-up delinquent and speed freak who booms down the interstates in his 18-wheeler as if he were tooling a Formula One car around the bricks at Indianapolis. He spends his time listening to CB reports of Smokeys, so he can keep rolling at 70 plus without getting flagged down by a patrolman.

Snort Johnson thinks of himself as a Marlboro man, but what he smokes is "wacky tobaccy"— stuff that spaces him out, slows his reactions in emergencies and distorts his depth perception.

Snort started by popping "uppers" so he could feel better and be more alert behind the wheel. But this became a habit that strung him out into a nervous wreck, a twitchy paranoid who shouldn't be wheeling a bicycle, much less a rig carrying gasoline or dangerous chemicals.

Luther Lushwell is the fella you see at the truck stop who knocks back a six-pack of beer before he climbs into his cab to hit the road, or anything else in his way. Lucky for him that his truck doesn't have 20 gears, because he's too boozed up to count that high without taking off his boots.

Lane Weaver makes travel risky for anyone driving in the same county. He dodges back and forth from lane to lane like a kid on a new motorcycle. He loves to ride your bumper while blasting you out of your seat with his air horn.

Randy Scofflaw is an unscrupulous hustler who is always scheming to make an extra buck by over-loading his truck. Sure, it's illegal. Sure, it hammers our highways into rubble, costing taxpayers millions. But what does Randy care, if there's a bigger pay-check at the other end? You can sometimes hear Randy and his buddies on CB, scheming how to slip around cargo checkpoints.

Dudley Doubleclutch is a scruffy type whose truck is an accident waiting to happen. Dudley's tires are thinner than the ham in a drugstore sandwich. His brakes couldn't stop a baby buggy that was roll-ing uphill.

Dudley's engine is a giant smudge pot, laying down a cloud of fumes that would make a skunk hold his nose. He's a one-man smog attack.

As long as these rogues are sharing our highways, we'll have to watch out for them. To be fair, how-ever, let's admit that we RVers have some space cases in our own ranks, drivers who give truckers a bad time. Driving an RV out of a rest area at 10 miles an hour into the path of a highballing 18-wheeler, for example, is no way to improve any trucker's disposi-tion. But I'll say this — I have yet to see a motor-home tailgating a truck.

Catching the Mighty RONCACHO

AS WE CAMPED ALONG woodland streams in the Northwest on our first RV summer, I began seeing strange-looking creatures flitting through the trees. They looked like Sasquatch — that mysterious, man-like creature that some people swear they've seen in the deep woods.

I tried sneaking up on one and got glimpses of it waddling along on strange, rubbery appendages, like a walrus. It had feathers all over its chest and a thick mat of bushy fur on its face. Oddest of all, it had a long antenna bobbing along in front of it. What could it be?

Suddenly the creature detected my presence and turned toward me, and I realized with a shock that it was human. It was, in fact, an RVer who was almost unrecognizable under several layers of fishing gear.

Those strange, rubbery appendages turned out to be hip boots, and the feathers were trout flies hooked onto a fishing vest. The bushy fur was a beard, and that antenna-like thing bobbing along in front of him was a fly casting rod.

Vastly relieved, I called out, "Hallooo! How's fishing?"

"The fishin's fine," he replied, "but the catchin's

not so good."

He stared at me in puzzlement and asked, "Where's your fishin' outfit?"

I could have told him how I lost my tackle battling a 90-pound Dolly Varden that chased me back to camp, but only real fishermen can lie like that and get away with it. So I confessed: "I don't fish."

I must say he took it like a man. He swayed a bit, grabbed a tree for support and then gave me an incredulous, pitying look, as though I had said I'd never kissed anybody but my sister.

I got that same look from many another RV sports fisherman or woman whenever we chanced to park in trout country. There they'd all be, standing around outside their rigs in their waders and such, trading outrageous fish stories, while I slunk around in jogging shoes and a windbreaker — and pants, of course — trying to look inconspicuous. I began to realize that I'd never be a genuine outdoors RVer until I could bend a rod with the best of them.

It's not that I've never wanted to fish. I've long had a love-hate relationship with the sport. I love the idea of fishing, but hate what happens whenever I try it.

I once took a trip to the little fishing village of San Felipe, on Mexico's Baja Peninsula. A writer friend, John Reese, asked me along to go after totuava, an enormous fish that John said usually weighs a couple of hundred pounds. I believed it when we chartered a Mexican fisherman's boat and saw those massive trolling rods with line the size of cable wound on reels like winches. Ah, this would be real sport!

I did land several fish, but none of them were to-tuavas. The captain identified them all as *roncachos*. I had never heard of *roncachos,* but evidently the waters of Baja were teeming with these ugly little things. I was glad when the captain tossed them over the side, which meant I wouldn't have to clean or eat them.

After we returned to port, I asked John about *roncachos*. He was immediately seized with a mysterious fit of merriment and began rolling around on the floor. When he could talk again, he informed me that there was no such fish as a roncacho. What the captain had been telling me, in his fractured English, was that my fish was a "wrong catch."

The Baja junket was admittedly embarrassing, but the experience I'd really like to forget came when my neighbor, Good Ole Walt, offered to take me on a charter boat out of San Pedro to fish for albacore. I felt pretty salty as we left the harbor, watching the fish leap out of the water.

But after we sailed beyond the breakwater and slammed into those big ocean rollers, it was our boat that started leaping out of the water. It rolled and staggered, pitched and shuddered while I clung to the rail, and my stomach kept trying to jump overboard.

Walt gave me a concerned look. "You OK, Ray?"

"Sure," I lied.

"Then you better notify your face, buddy," said Walt, "because you look mighty green around the gills."

Moments later there was a tremendous commotion. I hoped it meant we'd struck a reef and would have to abandon ship. But no such luck. Instead, we had tied into a huge school of albacore. Some fool fish even hit on my lure by mistake, assuming I was a fisherman. I felt a heavy strike, and the reel sang with a high-pitched "zzzzzzzz" as the fish took off with my line.

"He's a whopper," shouted Good Ole Walt. "Reel him in!"

I knew this was the Big Moment, but by now my knees were Jello, and the horizon was doing nip-ups. All I could do was hand Good Ole Walt the pole and mumble, "You take him."

Then I staggered off to go below deck and lay face down on a bunk. I stayed there, breathing the reek of gasoline fumes for several eternities, until the guys upstairs — I mean on deck — had hauled in a whole boat load of fish. It was everybody else's best day in years.

By the time we got back inside the breakwater, my stomach was making more revolutions than the ship's propeller. They bury people who feel better than I did. But when Good Ole Walt showed our neighbors the big fish "we" caught, he never let on what had really happened. That's how a guy earns a name like Good Ole Walt.

I finally did some real fishing in British Columbia. We ferried our motorhome to Vancouver Island and chartered a small boat, captained by the owner of Camp Costa Lotta — honest, that's the name of the place. The salmon were running, so Captain Ken took a fellow RVer and me out trolling one late afternoon.

Captain Ken rigged the trolling lines down about 28 feet, and then explained how to play a fish by snubbing the reel with the friction of your palm. We had a strike within minutes, and Ken handed me the pole. The odd thing is that I remembered to do everything right, and landed a 9-pound spring salmon. I was elated. But one catch doth not a fisherman make, as I learned when a much bigger salmon hit my lure. He leaped high out of the water to show us he was at least a 25-pounder, and then zizzzzed off with my line so fast that I forgot to snub the reel — and got a snarled line instead of a salmon.

Fortunately for my morale, which now was lower than a halibut's belly, I got another hookup. I did everything right again, landing a 9-pound coho that put up quite a fight. As darkness came, my fellow RVer caught another 9-pounder.

Catching those salmon finally did it to me. I fell for fishing — hook, line and sinker. I'm already thinking about heading back down to Baja for a fine mess of Roncachos.

A Dog's Life in an RV
By
Charlie the Poodle

THERE'S NOTHING LIKE riding down the open road in an RV with your nose out the window, ears flapping in the breeze, watching the countryside go by. When you've had enough scenery, you can always sneak up on the sofa to relax, or take a nap under the dinette until kibble time.

Best of all, when you arrive somewhere, it's not like the old neighborhood, with the same dumb cats you've chased a hundred times. No, it's a whole new world of open meadows, giant trees and leafy trails with a thousand exciting scents you've never sniffed before and furry creatures scampering everywhere.

Time was when a city dog with adventure in his soul would have to run away from home to enjoy such pleasures. The price was high — sleeping in alleys on cold, rainy nights, and scrounging for scraps of food while dodging cars and dog catchers.

But dogs today have it made. We can travel aboard an RV in pampered luxury, with a cook and chauffeur. If that's a dog's life, I'll bet a lot of humans would like to trade places.

As any pet knows, however, nothing is perfect

when you have to depend on human beings. There'll be times when you're ready for a romp, but your owner just keeps driving and driving, trying to reach some faraway place before sundown. You're dying to stretch your legs, but there's nothing to do but snooze and scratch. What to do?

First I put my nose in the driver's lap to get his attention. Then I do my show and tell number, running to the side door and scratching to get out. If that fails, I whimper as if I can't possibly hold on another minute. That never fails. My owner panics and slams on the brakes when I do that.

Incidentally, that run-for-the-door-with-a-frantic-look routine is also handy in case your owners buy dog food that you don't like. If this happens to you, and you find some yucky cheapo gunk in your dinner bowl, don't just put your tail between your legs and give up. Instead, pretend to eat some, and then run to the door every fifteen minutes or so with an urgent look on your face. Your owner will get the picture in a hurry and say, "This new food sure doesn't agree with that poor dog. We'd better go back to the stuff he likes."

You need to know humans like the back of your paw if you want to get the most out of RVing. For example, there's no sense getting excited when your owners go out wearing bathrobes and carrying towels. They're headed for a shower, not a walk.

But if you see them putting on jogging shoes, or hats and coats, that's your cue to let them know you want to go along. Wagging your tail and frisking around usually gets the message across. But if it doesn't, use your imagination. Play Lassie and fetch your leash. If it still looks as if they'll leave you be-hind, put them on a guilt trip by hanging your head and drooping your ears. That'll get them.

If you're new to RV's, I'd like to pass along some important advice. There's an old human saying, "Look before you leap"— and that applies to us dogs, too. Don't just go scrambling out the door in a strange RV park; you never know what's out there. I've run into everything from Japanese Akita dogs twice my size to enormous animals called bears that are very bad news.

You might also encounter some treacherous ani-mals with stripes down their backs that look like cats, but aren't. If you chase one of these woods pussies, it'll spray you with awful smelling stuff that will tie your nose in a knot for weeks.When your owner takes you to the desert, beware of plants called cactus. The worst ones for us dogs are shaped like fireplugs, but believe me, they're more like porcupines. I sniffed one once and got a nose full of needles. (But it could have been worse. I'm just lucky I always sniff before I spritz.)

One of the best things about an RV dog's life is that you get to meet a lot of other interesting canine travelers, like that foxy French poodle named Fifi that I met in Vegas. I don't want to sound immodest, but that sexy little number was all over me in seconds with that "let's-have-puppies" look in her eyes. I got so excited, I forgot I'd been fixed.

Unfortunately, the lady who owns Fifi spotted us and snatched her away, ending our attempted entan-glement. Ever since then, whenever an RV like Fifi's goes by, I wonder if she's aboard and thinking of me.

Oh, well, *c'est la vie.*

By the way, if Fifi's owner happens to be reading this, I'd love to hear from her. Maybe Fifi and I could get together over a box of Yummies and yap a while about our summer romance. My intentions are strictly honorable. Well, fairly honorable. Well, what difference does it make when you're fixed?

Scenery You
Don't Dare See

WHY IS IT THAT MOTHER Nature puts her best scenery along the worst stretches of road where a driver doesn't dare look? You spend all that money on a trailer or motorhome to enjoy the sights, and what do you see in the most famous places? Narrow lanes with blind corners. Steep descents into horseshoe curves. Wriggly warning signs, hinting all kinds of potential disasters.

Meanwhile your companion is ooing and ahhing over mountain peaks, river gorges or coastal vistas far below as you stare grimly ahead, knuckles whitening on the steering wheel, intent on survival.

It's enough to make a grown man wish he could buy something like an Automatic Scenery Recorder to save the sights for later, after his heart leaves his throat.

I could have used an ASR when my wife suggested that we drive our motorhome down Highway 1 along the Northern California coastline, south of Mendocino.

The natural beauty of Highway 1 is world-renowned, but the road itself is a two-lane, serpentine stretch of bad news, often shrouded in dense fog, with more switchbacks than the Himalayas. I protested to Ethel that I'd driven that road before in a sports car, and it would scare the beard off a mountain goat. (No wonder mountain goats have white hair.) But she had her heart set on seeing that spectacular coastline from atop the bluffs.

She claims there was a fabulous sunset when we came snaking through there, but I wouldn't know. All I saw were tight turns, zigzags and drop-offs with no safety rails to prevent us from cartwheeling down into the ocean. I felt like I was driving a dynamite truck in an old Humphrey Bogart movie.

Meanwhile, Ethel grew strangely silent. She just sat there, the color of a marshmallow, as the rear wheels of our 35-foot vehicle kept scraping the gravelly cliff edge on sharp turns. If I so much as glanced at the ocean, she'd shriek, "Don't look!"

I didn't see enough scenery that afternoon to make a post card. But if somebody had invented an Automatic Scenery Recorder, I could have watched it all on our TV set that night.

As a gadget lover, I carry a weather radio that picks up the nearest U.S. Weather Service transmitter, no matter where we happen to be. It even lights up and sounds off whenever there's a weather alert. Now, it seems to me that some bright computer whiz could use those broadcast alerts to trigger another device RVers need — an Automatic Storm Batten-Downer.

Let's suppose you're parked somewhere for a picnic, and your radio starts beeping to warn that a major storm is headed your way. If you had an Automatic Storm Batten-Downer, you wouldn't have to dash outside and roll up the awning before it blew away, or get a bath when it dumped a barrel's worth of rain down your neck. The awning would roll itself up, the windows would shut themselves, and your VCR would click on with a good movie for a rainy afternoon.

Another invention that Ethel and I could use in our motorhome is a Diet-O-Matic, a device to scan our dinner plates, calculate the calories, and, if necessary, slap a time lock on the refrigerator, so we couldn't stuff our faces between meals.

If you travel with a dog or cat, then you probably know why we'd like to have an Automatic Lie Detector for Wayward Pets. Our dogs are brazen fibbers, but we can never prove it.

One night we returned to our motorhome and found that one or both dogs had polished off the sirloin we were thawing for dinner, plus a big bowl of fruit, leaving nothing but banana skins behind.

"Charlie,' I said to the poodle, "did you climb up on the stove and swipe that steak?" He looked me right in the eye, innocent as an altar boy, as if to say, "Who, me?"

Ethel stared accusingly at Lena the Doberman, who goes wild at the scent of bananas. "Did you eat all that fruit, you naughty girl?" Lena turned her head away shyly, but I'd swear I heard a snicker.

We gave up grilling this hardened pair of prevaricators, but if we'd had an Automatic Lie Detector for Wayward Pets, I could have slapped the electronic paw-cuffs on them and found out who was committing what.

The problem I'd like most to solve with computer automation involves my running battle with drain hoses. I've wasted many an hour fumbling around with hoses that either don't reach or don't fit the pipes in whatever campground we've chosen for the night.

What I need is a Robotic Drain Seeker — a high-tech hose that will snake out of our motorhome on command, sniffing around until it locates and locks onto the proper drainpipe. Meanwhile, I could be sitting inside, warm and dry, pushing buttons and quaffing a light beer.

I understand such a gadget is already under development, but they're still working the bugs out of it. The first model of the Robotic Drain Seeker became confused during a test run when a camper came by who'd just spent two weeks in the woods without a bath. You can guess what happened when it got a whiff of *him*. I'm told it wrapped its coils around him like some man-eating plant, then tried to lock on, never mind how, so it could fill him with 20 gallons of dishwater.

Meanwhile, he was yelling and wriggling, trying to prevent the RDS from homing in for a connection. I understand he is now fully recovered, the only after-effect being a tendency to blow soapy bubbles whenever he gets excited.

Potatoes à la Couch

WHEN WE FIRST BOUGHT our motorhome, we had a blissful case of the "gonna be's." We promised ourselves we were gonna be leading a healthier life through diet and exercise. We were gonna be out on the trail every morning in our jogging outfits, or pedaling our bikes down country lanes. We did that, and it was great fun, but when the rainy weather came, we stopped doing it as often.

What we didn't stop doing was eating. By the time I decided I'd better get back to exercising, I couldn't buckle the belt on my jogging shorts. Rather than let Ethel know of this embarrassing predicament, I switched to an old pair of sweat pants that have a simple drawstring at the waist. My previous waist disappeared, replaced by a vague and deceptive shapelessness.

Meanwhile, Ethel was getting more exercise trying to squeeze into her clothes than most people get at a gym. (As Ethel says, "It's not easy to look like Julia Roberts when you eat like Roseanne Barr.") Ethel's problem was trying to wrestle the zipper up on her exercise shorts. And when she did manage to pull it up by holding her breath, it promptly zipped down again of its own accord. Since we were not parked on a nude beach, this was a crisis.

What did us in? Other than our willpower, which crumbled like fresh oatmeal cookies at the sight of food? I'd say it was the seductive convenience of motorhome living. Where is there greater temptation than in a motorhome, where a well-stocked refrigerator is literally within arm's reach of the dining table? A person could gain three pounds in one night without ever getting up.

We soon discovered that the road to hell is paved with good inventions like the freezer. Ours was stuffed with pastries that we'd consume a la mode. We couldn't have gained weight faster if we'd had a 50-gallon tub of ice cream and automatic spoons.

Before motorhomes, travelers were lucky to find a decent piece of pie to go with muddy coffee at a roadside diner. Now, we can cram a zillion calories into our freezers, and eat ourselves crazy.

The only real limitation on determined eaters is the danger of becoming Couch Potatoes. That's OK for a while, but as a lifestyle, it doesn't offer all that much.

One night, after dining with our dearest companions — Sara Lee and Haagen-Daz — we realized we were expanding like the national debt. If we'd ever hit the bathroom scales at the same time, we'd have smashed that sucker flat.

Even though Ethel looks great in khaki, she wasn't looking forward to buying her next dress in Sears' tent department. And I worried after hearing a doctor on TV say that blood pressure tends to rise with weight gain. I didn't want to end up taking those blood-pressure pills that sometimes cause impotence, whatever that is.

In a rush of willpower, we made a vow we'd eat no more ice cream until we'd each lost 15 pounds. Then, to make sure there would be no ice cream around to tempt us, we got out the last quart of French vanilla and polished it off.

Life went on like that until the day when we got to talking with two of our slimmest friends of the road, Nancy and David Wynne of Maine. Nancy is quite attractive and as slender as a young girl. Handsome, white bearded David is as trim as a youth half his age.

We wondered how they did it. Did they have high metabolism, like hummingbirds? Or did they just eat like birds? What was their secret?

"Pritikin," they said. "We follow the Pritikin diet and eat practically no fats." Well, I didn't want to insult them, but I'd long suspected that Pritikin was depriving his brain as well as his body.

Nancy and David didn't do a hard sell on us. They weren't evangelistic, menu-thumping Pritikin's Witnesses as one might expect. But they were powerful apostles for the good life of diet and exercise, and seeing is believing.

When you look at a married couple your own age, and see them clear-eyed and fit, full of energy and eager for whatever adventure comes next, you know they're doing something right. And you want to be like they are.

I read one of Pritikin's paperbacks, and discovered that he does not urge his followers to burn down the bakeries, candy shops or meat markets. He doesn't insist they eat nothing but bean sprouts and tofu on a stick. He approves of lean meat, in unlimited amounts. And he insists on vigorous exercise, which he considers crucial to a healthy way of life.

We'd heard about the dramatic case histories of Pritikin graduates, people who could barely totter in the door, then charging back out after a month or so of lifestyle changes, like tigers reborn. Having nothing to lose but flab and cellulite, we decided to go for a plate or two of Pritikin.

Soon we were indeed losing weight, while simultaneously confronting one of the great mysteries of dieting: Why does Mother Nature always remove those hard-lost pounds from exactly the wrong places?

As soon as Ethel started to lose weight, it all came off upstairs. You could practically hear her bra slowly crumpling after every meal, yet her skirt hung on until the last.

Once we really made up our minds to get fit and trim, our motorhome became our ally, taking us to mountain trails and sandy beaches, where we could jog and build endurance. Even our dogs became lean and charged with energy as they raced up and down the shore at Homer Spit in Alaska, and below the cliffs along the wild and beautiful shores of Oregon. We rode our mountain bikes through the woods of Washington, and down along the bikeways of Venice, California, dodging the roller skaters and skateboarders.

The very first night we Pritikined, in British Columbia, we pedaled home from a vigorous outing to find that our next-door neighbors in the park were barbecuing hamburgers. The smell of roasting patties was absolutely dizzying as we sat down to a modest

salad with lemon dressing. We nibbled herbivorously
while the barbecue blazed away with its maddening
aromas just below our window. We could see our
neighbors stuffing their faces with whole platters of
hot, juicy burgers. It was torture.

We might never have survived without running
amok in a meat market if it hadn't been for our RV's
combination microwave/convection oven. The real
wonder of this machine is its ability to "sensor cook."
You put a dish of veggies in a covered plate, push a
button, and it cooks to perfection, shutting the
power off at just the right moment. Sensor-cooked
vegetarian meals are easy to fix, low in calories and
utterly delicious. Steak and fries they're not. But as
veggies go, they are marvelous.

How did we do as dieters? We gave the Pritikin
approach a good effort, and each lost nearly 15
pounds in two months. Unfortunately we then fell
from grace, nibbling no-no's as the pounds slipped
back on, inch by shameful inch. It is one of the more
melancholy truths of life that food is "a moment on
the lips, and a lifetime on the hips." So now we're
back to watching our fat intake again, Pritikin-style.
And it's working. Let's hear it for non-fat French vanilla.

Strictly Personal

SINCE I AM A WRITER, people tend to assume that I know something about the world, beyond the fact that it is round and a great place to explore in an RV.

Several RVers have been desperate enough to write to me, of all people, for advice. I may not know all the answers, but my wife says I'm the least reluctant person she knows to give an opinion.

So, with apologies to Dear Abby, let's dip once more into the mailbag.

Q: *I thought my husband's interest in you-know-what would calm down after he retired and bought a motorhome, but he's having so much fun traveling around that he's like a kid again. Isn't you-know-what a strain on an older man's heart?*

A: The latest studies show exercise, including you-know-what, is good for most older people. If you're worried about your husband's heart, consider having him examined by a doctor. You might also try to get him interested in other sports or hobbies besides you-know-what. But, you know what? Maybe you're just tired of all that you-know-what-ting. Try telling him you need some bed rest.

PS. What do you feed him?

Q: *We love our big shaggy dog and always take him on trips, but we can't keep him off the couch. Any suggestions?*

A: We used to have the same trouble with Lena, our comfort-loving Doberman, who'd sneak up there after the lights were out. Then I read somewhere about scattering several mousetraps on a couch to scare off a pet, so we tried it.

Sure enough, shortly after we went to bed, we heard the snappity-snap of several traps going off like a string of ladyfinger firecrackers. Lena yiped and hit the floor running. Ever had a nervous Doberman dive into bed with you? (No, the traps didn't hurt her.)

The following night, when I got up for a glass of milk, I forgot the traps and sat on them myself. What happened? I yiped, hit the floor running, and dove into bed with Ethel.

Q: *Recently my husband took off on a fishing weekend with some buddies, and left me all alone in our RV. That night I met a real friendly bachelor gentleman in the campground laundromat.*

One thing led to another, and the next thing I knew, we were in his RV, drinking Bud Lite and laughing and having a wonderful time. To tell the truth, we had so much beer, I can't remember everything that happened. Did I do wrong?

A: Well, you certainly had every opportunity.

Q: *My husband and I have just become full-timers. What do you suggest for staying healthy on the road?*

A: Here are a few simple recommendations:

1. Walk your dog (and/or mate) every day if possible. Walks are a wonderful way for RVers to enjoy the countryside and keep healthy at the same time. (Don't be like some folks whose idea of exercise is getting off the couch to change channels.)

2. Take it easy on fatty foods. If your RV's tires go flat, you're overdoing it.

3. Never eat anything from your RV refrigerator that you don't personally recognize. I once made a meat loaf sandwich of "leftovers" that turned out to be dog food. I was very upset to find this out, and so was the dog.

Q: *My husband wears dentures, and has a bald spot and a pot belly, but he still thinks he's God's gift to women. How can I keep the old goat from constantly talking to other females?*

A: Hide his teeth.

Q: *What do you think of sex on the road?*

A: I don't recommend sex on the road. You might get run over. Stay in your motorhome where it's cozy, safe and private — and stop thinking like a chipmunk.

Heading for the Showers

SOMETIMES I ENVY THOSE organized characters who show up at RV park washrooms in monogrammed bathrobes and leather sandals, carrying their neat little toiletry kits. They make showering look so easy. They're in and out in no time, clean, fresh and faultlessly groomed, while I'm still standing on one foot like a flamingo, trying to wriggle into clean clothes without getting them wet.

Often as not, I lose my balance and go plunging out in the midst of the guys who are shaving, with my shorts at half-mast. I just don't have the knack of showering in washrooms without making a public spectacle of myself.

I also envy RVers who shower in their own rigs. We have a shower, but if we used it, we'd have no place to stuff the brooms, the barbecue, the dog kibble bucket and the laundry. (The only one who gets to shower in our motorhome is the poodle, and that's because parks don't allow him to bathe with the bipeds.)

After taking showers in RV parks all over North America, I've become rather paranoid about turning on the water in a new place for the first time. I'll never forget the morning in Anchorage when, unknown to me, a workman had accidentally left the main hot water valve shut off.

After adjusting the cold tap, I turned the hot water lever on full force — and was blasted with a glacial stream that would freeze the speckles off a trout. It was so cold, I couldn't even yell. I came close to a cryogenic experience — the kind where scientists freeze your corpus in hopes of thawing you out in the distant future.

The next morning, I made sure it wouldn't happen again. I turned the *hot* water on first — and out spat an angry gusher so hot you could pluck a chicken with it and still have enough steam left over to press a size fifty suit.

One particularly tricky shower I encountered in San Diego would gladden a miser's heart. It had a water-saving lever that you had to keep holding down to get any water whatever, which meant showering with one hand. There's not much to be said for one-handed showering unless you are behind in your yoga. It tends to leave you with soap streaks in unreachable places.

Equally frustrating was a push-button shower which would pop back off every few seconds before I could even get wet. After going a few rounds with this hostile gizmo, I needed a cold shower just to cool off.

But until I went to British Columbia this summer, I'd never seen the ultimate threat, a pay shower. I remember stumbling into a handsomely tiled washroom one morning, half-asleep. I stripped down and turned the water handle in all the usual directions, but nothing happened.

Then I spotted the new thing — a shiny metal

box on the wall. The instructions said to insert a quarter for five minutes worth of shower. All right, thought I, fumbling through my pants for a quarter, but there was no quarter to be found.

I put my clothes back on and set out to get change. Naturally, the office wasn't open yet, so I had to hike back to the motorhome to ask Ethel if she had any quarters.

"Yes," she said, "but I'll need them all for the laundry."

I managed to wheedle one quarter out of her by promising to get more change later, and returned to the shower. I stripped down again, dropped in my quarter, water gushed out, I fine-tuned the stream to the exact temperature I wanted, and soaped up, relaxing at last in the steamy luxury of it all.

But as I started to rinse down, there was an ominous, pipe-rattling "chunggggg!" The five minutes were up, and the water had cut off. There I stood, wreathed in shampoo and soapsuds, with not a dribble of water to be had.

As I stood there, puckering, I pondered my predicament. Obviously I should have brought *two* quarters. Or worn a waterproof watch with a sweep second hand, so I wouldn't get caught with my suds on. Now all I could do was rinse off in the sink — a demeaning thought — or go get another quarter.

Aha! Since Ethel was doubtless in the laundry room by now, next door to the showers, I decided I could slip in there and get another quarter.

But when I padded barefoot into the laundry room, wearing naught but a towel around my waist, there was no Ethel. There was, instead, a proper middle-aged Canadian lady who was folding laundry. As she turned and saw me, she did quite a take. Not wishing to create an international incident, I sought to explain my semi-nudity:

"I thought my wife was here doing laundry," I said.

"Indeed," said the lady. She stepped back a pace, looking uneasily at this apparition from the men's shower.

"I just came in for a quarter," I said.

"You want me to give you a quarter?" She edged further away.

"Oh, no," I said. "I thought you were my wife."

"Your wife?"

"I mean, she's supposed to be here, and I need a quarter for the shower."

"Oooh," said the lady. She pointed to a bill-changing machine on the wall. "You can get change from that machine. You do have a dollar, do you not?"

"Not on me," I said. "I'd better get my pants."

"Yes, do," she replied.

For once, luck was with me. I found a Canadian dollar crumpled in a pants pocket and hurried back to the laundry room. The lady eyed me narrowly as I slipped the dollar into the changer.

The machine promptly burped the bill back out, perhaps because the dollar was so wrinkled that Queen Elizabeth looked more like Queen Victoria.

At this point, my wife showed up with our laundry and stared at the towel-clad me in some surprise.

"What are you doing in here like that?" she asked.

"Looking for you," I replied. "I need a quarter."

"What happened to the quarter I gave you?"

"Never mind," said I, feeling some irritation and a cold draft. "Just gimme a dollar for the changer."

So she did, the machine accepted it, and I kept *two* of the quarters, just to be on the safe side. By now, the soap had dried on my skin, and I was in a rush to rinse off. Too rushed, as it turned out, because in my haste to pop a quarter into the timing machine, the mechanism jammed.

I pounded on the timer to make it cough up the quarter, whereupon my *second* quarter popped out of my fist and rolled away, out of sight, into the next stall.

I got down on my hands and knees to see where the coin had gone, and found myself peering at two hairy feet that belonged either to a gorilla or a linebacker.

I didn't want to risk pawing around under there, lest I grab this hulk's extremities by mistake, causing him to misread my intentions. Rather than humiliating myself further by asking the gorilla for my quarter, I took what seemed the easiest way out. I put on my towel and marched back to the laundry room.

"Now what?" asked Ethel.

"I don't want to talk about it. Just give me a quarter."

Ethel sighed. "What have they got in that men's room — video games?

"Just gimme the quarter, damn it!"

"Okay, Mr. Grumpy, okay."

This time, all finally went well. I inserted the quarter as carefully as a heart surgeon doing an implant, and the water came on. I rinsed down in great haste, before the pipes could go *chunggg* again.

As I came out of the shower, a man built like a Sequoia was combing his hair at the sink. He grinned in friendly fashion and, brandishing a quarter — obviously *my* quarter — he said, "I just had a free shower. Found this on the floor in there."

Did I ask him to return my quarter? No. There are times in life when it's wise to quit while you're behind. I learned that years ago, after getting cleaned in Las Vegas.

Eau de Diesel
& Essence of Cattle Truck

As a gadgeteer, I'm always on the lookout for any little gizmos that will enhance life aboard an RV. One of the latest is a fragrance dispenser that plugs into your cigar lighter. It sounds sensible, since a lot of things can happen in a RV, not all of them fragrant.

Let us suppose:

1.The man aboard is addicted to cheap Stogies that can wilt a Ponderosa at 100 yards. Or —

2. Your freezer conks out just when it's stuffed to overflowing with Rocky Mountain trout. Or —

3. You're caught in rush-hour trafic, assailed by such familiar interstate aromas as Eau de Diesel and Essence of Cattle Truck. Or —

4. The guarantee runs out on your holding tank.

With a fragrance dispenser on board, all you need do is press a button, and shazam! — instant relief. Your swooning schnoz is bathed in the fragrance of mountain pines.

Another handy gadget is an automatic car finder. It was invented for parking amnesiacs like me who leave their vehicles in some huge lot at a stadium or department store, and return to realize they can't find them amid thousands of other machines, all looking alike.

I remember the morning we left our RV in San Diego and drove the pickup to Disneyland. We got there so early that the parking lot was almost empty. But by the time we were ready to leave, our car had been swallowed up in a vast sea of metal.

The subsequent conversation, with expletives deleted, went something like this:

Wife: "Didn't you notice where we parked?"

Husband: "I thought I did, but I didn't. Did you?"

Wife: "Why should I? You were driving."

Husband: "What's that got to do with it?"

Wife: "Why is it you can never take the blame for anything?"

Husband: (Deleted, including gestures.)

We plodded up and down the rows for an hour or more, feeling dumber than Dopey and thoroughly Grumpy.

Evidently there are lots of us who could use the car-finder, a miniature key-chain transmitter that signals your car to honk its horn and flash its lights. Great idea, right?

But I wonder how I'd react when walking past somebody's car as all that blaring and flashing erupted, blasting me out of my shoes. I can see the coroner's verdict — "Death due to failure of auto immune system."

I like alarms in theory, but in real life they are much too alarming. The first night after we installed a burglar alarm system in our home, I wandered off to the bathroom, half-asleep, passing unaware through a sentry beam. The alarm system went crazy with a deafening clanging of bells that sounded like a prison breakout.

Bells that loud are absolutely paralyzing. I stood rooted to the carpet, heart hammering and every nerve twitching, until I finally realized what was happening. Then I fumbled vainly with the strange new controls while lights went on throughout the neighborhood, and people appeared on doorsteps in their pajamas.

I couldn't have gotten more attention if I'd been out in the street in my birthday suit, yelling "The Martians are coming." What looked like Martians did show up, waving guns and flashlights, but they turned out to be security guards who were annoyed to be rousted out by a false alarm.

Another gadget you might want in your RV is an electronic Garfield the Cat bathroom scale. Step on Garfield's face and his eyes pop open, and the scale gives you the bad news on its digital readout. I understand the principle quite well, since my eyes also pop open when I see the scales.

If you're not in the mood for Garfield, there's a similar machine featuring Miss Piggy. I just wouldn't have the nerve to bring it home.

Custom Canines

WHAT RVERS REALLY need are designer dogs — pets especially designed for the RV life. By designer dogs I don't mean those fancy-schmancy Gucci poochies that swagger through Beverly Hills and Manhattan with their manicured nails and $100 hairdos. I mean a real pet, scientifically bred by canine experts for the RV life-style.

It makes sense when you consider that our modern dogs were themselves bred for specific purposes. Shepherd dogs were developed through the centuries to herd sheep and protect them from predators.

Retrievers were bred to fetch game birds, and hounds to follow the scent of foxes and wild game. Germany's Dr. Doberman crossed a Rottweiler terrier with a pinscher to create the highly intelligent and courageous Doberman pinscher, which can play any role that humans desire, ranging from loveable pet to ferocious guard dog.

Breeders have also "down-sized" dogs, like cars and RVs. Several breeds are available in what might be called deluxe, standard, compact and subcompact sizes.

Take the poodle, for example. The largest is the Royal, an impressive and distinguished animal about the size of an Afghan hound. Contrast the Royal with the Toy, which weighs but a few pounds. Same dog, but totally different packaging.

So if the experts can breed a dog to practically any size and temperament, why can't they custom-design dogs for RVs? The answer is that they can.

What would the ideal RV pet be like? Well, we would certainly want him to be big enough to romp with, but small enough to stay out from underfoot. Like everything else aboard an RV, he would be compact and practical — the most dog per ounce of fur.

He'd be eager for a walk whenever we were, but not require a 10-K run for exercise. He would be playful and frisky, yet calm enough to lie quietly when we felt like relaxing.

He'd have a healthy appetite to keep up his animal spirits, but not be so ravenous that he'd eat us out of motorhome or trailer.

Most of all, he would have to be readily adaptable, because an RV dog never knows what life will bring from one day to the next.

And, as long as we're redesigning the RV pet, he ought to have the bladder of a camel. (Many RVers' lives today are governed by how frequently their pets need to make pit stops.)

In these days of genetic engineering, gene-splicing, transplants and such, our chances of creating an ideal RV pet would seem to be better than ever. Some day, we'll be able to stroll into a Puppery, or whatever they'll call these places, and give the breeding designer a sketch with the exact specifications for the perfect pet.

It's hard to say how much breed redesigning is going on at this very moment. Breeders are apt to be very hush-hush when they are creating something new for the canine market. But I do have a few rumors and snippets of thoroughly unreliable information, based on reports from certain highly placed cage attendants in the major kennels of Europe. And while the new dogs in development are not specifically designed as yet for RV's, they show what might be done.

Imagine Germany's premiere breeder-geneticist hard at work creating a subminiature Dachshund called the Wurst, intended for people with small apartments. The Wurst would be about the length of a frankfurter, and approximately one mustard jar tall. Many believe it will be cute enough to eat, which may be why breeders expect it to be shy and rather high-strung.

The French may then follow suit by downsizing the poodle even further into a new Poodelle version, small enough to be carried in a lady's purse. Women with Poodelles in their handbags would no longer have to rummage around inside them, since these clever little canines could be trained to retrieve small objects like lipsticks and eyeliners.

Once the market develops for really small dogs, the Japanese can be expected to flood the United States with well-built minidogs that would require little upkeep or maintenance. Their basic, no-frills Yamahound would be an economical animal that could run for a week on a single milkbone.

Security-minded RV owners should be particularly interested in minidogs bred for protection as well as companionship. The Germans are said to be developing the Dobermite, eight ounces of pure guard dog. The secret weapon of the Dobermite would be its incredibly loud bark, intended to frighten any intruder into thinking that the dog in question is the size of a mastiff.

Britain's proposed Pocket Terrier is described as a standard-looking terrier in miniature, designed to fit into a hip pocket. The thought here is that the closer a watchdog is to your wallet, the better. The Germans are said to be developing a similar animal, the Wallet Weimeraner. When a pickpocket reaches for your wallet, this feisty little beast goes straight for his knuckles.

Meanwhile, Mexican breeders are thought to be working on a tiny guard dog for a lady to tuck down the front of her bra to discourage unwanted attentions. This dog is the Chihbrahua.

Now that gene splicers are experimenting with breeding across species lines, I would like to suggest some *really* new and unique creatures especially for RVers. One is the Puffhound, a cross between a miniature guard dog and a puffer fish. When danger threatened, the Puffhound would puff itself up to the size of a Great Dane.

I'd like to see breeders cross a dog and a chameleon, producing a canine that could change colors. It would be invaluable whenever you arrived at an RV park where dogs were not allowed. If your pet were a Dogameleon, you could simply command the animal to disappear — and it would camouflage itself, becoming invisible to park attendants.

These are but a few thoughts about the exciting

prospects for custom canines. I think I'll put my orders in for one Dobermite, two Pocket Terriers and one purse-dwelling Poodelle for my wife, who can never find her lipstick.

The Same to You, Fella!

AFTER WE D BEEN ON THE road for a while, I realized I'd better become handy with tools. Or at least learn their names, and which end of what does the work.

I had always intended to master tools, but never got the hang of it. I still have trouble hammering anything, unless you count thumbs. What's worse, I never get a chance to make my toolish mistakes in private. The moment I bring out the RV toolbox, a crowd shows up to snicker and point fingers.

I could be miles from anywhere on an old burro trail in the middle of the Mojave Desert, and as soon as I picked up a pair of pliers, fifty people would pop up like jackrabbits out of the sagebrush, pointing and snickering.

I'm in awe of RVers who carry a toolbox the size of a Minnie Winnie and can fix anything from a leaky transmission to a cranky commode. They seem to have memorized the manual for every rig on the road. How do they do that? Why are they puttering around RV parks, when they could be running the Pentagon motor pool?

Inspired by the Super Fixers among us, I am re-solving once more when New Year's rolls around to become better with my toolbox, even if it 's only to get it open on the first try.

While I'm at it, my wife has suggested that I resolve to become a little less apoplectic on the road. I am therefore resolving not to lose my temper in situations such as when:

A reckless driver cuts me off, then gives me a digital salute, a gesture known to highway psychologists as "flipping the bird."

Tailgaters snuggle up to my back bumper and blast the wax out of my ears with their airhorns.

I follow the signs to a scenic drive and find nothing to look at but a paving crew that has traffic blocked off in both directions.

We go through the same city three times because I can't find the turn off out of town.

I coast up to a gas station with a near-empty tank and see a sign that says, "Unleaded only."

The air-conditioner picks Las Vegas in July to quit running.

I have also promised my wife that I will try to forego using those expletives still lingering from my days in the military when:

I trip in the dark and dump a stack of wooden wheel chocks on my toes.

I unlock a storage compartment and get buried in an avalanche of off-season clothes, racquets and fishing gear.

Our sofa bed for guests suddenly flattens out as I'm tugging at it, catapulting me backward across the aisle.

The door jams shut and I have to wriggle through a window to get inside.

The heater quits on a three-dog night in Alaska.

Our shore-power connection won't fit a park's outlets, and all my adapter plugs are safely stored back home.

Our outside waterhose connector blows off in the middle of the night, flooding the campground.

A party coach comes barreling in at midnight with a load of half-deaf rock 'n' rollers.

We run out of supplies in the boonies, and Sunday dinner becomes a peanut butter sandwich.

That huge beast heard prowling around in the dark all night turns out to be a squirrel with insomnia.

This year I am also resolving to keep my cool, no matter what happens on the road. I figure just about everything that can happen to us already has, except a hijacking.

I wouldn't be surprised if some elderly lady boards our motorhome at a stop light some day, pulls a derringer from her knitting bag and says, "Start drivin', Sonny. We're goin' to Florida!"

Canadians to the Rescue

IT WAS THE BEST OF DAYS and the worst of days. The best because we were atop the mountain on Salt Spring Island, off the coast of British Columbia, enjoying one of the finest views in all of North America. But it was also the worst of days, because our beloved Charlie, the mischievous standard poodle, chose that beautiful fall afternoon to run off into the woods and disappear.

We had left our motorhome in a pleasantly wooded RV park on Vancouver Island, and driven our pickup onto a small ferry for an overnight visit to Salt Spring, the largest of Canada's Gulf Islands. Ethel and I were jammed into the front seat with our vacationing daughter, Caroline. Charlie and Lena, our Doberman rode in the back.

I suppose all RVers who travel with pets share the same worry lurking in the back of their minds. Some day their pet may suddenly bolt out the door in some remote area, and never be seen again.

It happened when we reached the summit and Ethel opened the passenger door. Charlie came bounding through the back window onto Ethel's lap, using her for a trampoline as he streaked off into the woods. Lena was right behind him. Within seconds, both dogs had disappeared in the deep woods. Fortu-

nately, Lena had stayed within earshot. She came
bounding back when we shouted her name.

But not Charles. We called him again and again,
but there was only silence. Unfortunately, the mountainside was not only heavily forested, but rocky and
slippery from the rains. Ethel and Caroline wanted to
go down the slope to look for him, but that seemed
rather risky, since the mountainside dropped off toward the ocean, and we had no idea how steep it
was.

We tramped back and forth over the immediate
area, calling for Charles until we were hoarse. Finally,
as the sun was going down and heavy rains came
pelting down again, we gave up and drove back our
bed-and-breakfast chalet for the night

None of us got much sleep worrying about Charlie. I kept picturing our city-bred standard poodle
wandering in the chill darkness, wet to the skin, shivering, thirsty and hungry. Next morning we told our
hosts, Pearl and Malcolm Graham, that we wanted to
stay over so we could resume our search. They told
us they'd been planning to close the place for several
days so they could visit their son's family on Vancouver Island. But rather than turn us away at a time like
this, the Grahams said, "You just stay here. We'll
give you the keys, and you can lock up whenever
you leave."

We gratefully accepted, impressed yet again by
the generosity and friendliness of Canadians. Our
friend Anne Watson, a local real-estate agent, helped
us get organized the next day. She gave us maps and
suggested we notify the Royal Canadian Mounted
Police, as well as the Society for the Prevention of

Cruelty to Animals (SPCA). She also arranged for her husband, a school principal, to ask all the island children to be on the lookout for a big white poodle. The Mounties lent us a bullhorn. "I've owned a standard poodle myself," said one officer. "They're tough and they're smart. He'll probably be all right." Like other islanders we met on our search, he seemed convinced that Charlie would find his way down the mountain and be spotted as soon as he reached the main road.

SPCA officer Christine Wooldridge was similarly optimistic, but warned us that sheep ranchers along the lower road were tired of stray dogs that went after their flocks. One rancher had threatened to shoot any strange dog on sight. Shoot Charles? The idea was truly frightening.

We jumped into the truck and raced for the lower road. Then we went door to door, telling ranchers about Charles and offering a reward for his safe return. Afterward we cruised slowly up and down every road and byway on that side of the island, stopping everybody we met to tell them about him.

Rain was falling steadily, and our hearts sank with the setting sun, because Charles would now be spending his second night in the cold, dank wilderness without food or water. How long could he survive? Clearly, we would have to go back up the mountain and sweep the whole wooded area, top to bottom, until we found him. Fortunately, the Mounties said the slope wasn't too steep for hiking.

We got an early start next morning, resuming our hunt where we had last seen Charles. I couldn't climb because of an injured knee, so I dropped Ethel and Caroline off up top with the bullhorn. They combed through the area, heading downward while I cruised the lower road, scanning the mountainside with binoculars.

It was raining again, and eerily silent as Ethel and Caroline began picking their way down the boulder-strewn slope with Lena. Hours passed as they made their way through the forest, keeping in touch by shouting because the trees were so dense that they couldn't see one another.

I began to worry about them when they failed to show up on time below. They were more than an hour overdue when I finally heard a far-off voice yelling my name. I looked up to see Caroline in the distance, waving from a dirt road that led to the logging harbor.

"We've found him," she shouted. I just couldn't believe it. "Up here!" she yelled, beckoning for me to drive on up the narrow dirt access road. I joined her, and we soon caught up with an exhausted Ethel and a much-bedraggled, totally spent Charles being cared for by Pat St. Jean, a young woman living in an isolated home on the bay. Pat, an artist, was making tea for Ethel, who was slumped in a kitchen chair with Pat's shawl over her. At Ethel's feet was Charles, who lacked the strength even to wag his tail as I came inside.

Pat, one of those resourceful and totally self-reliant women you often meet in the Far North, went out to the woodshed and split some logs so she could build a comfortable fire.

"Lena found Charles," said Caroline. "She sud-

denly started pulling me sideways across the mountain, so fast I could hardly keep my feet.

"Then I saw this blob of white under a tree, not
moving. I yelled, 'Charles! Is that you?' but the blob
didn't move. And even when I came right up to him,
he barely lifted his head. It was as if he didn't even
recognize me." Ethel and Caroline had had quite a
time getting him down the mountain. Wherever they
could, they carried him. In other places, they coaxed
him along on his leash, with frequent stops so he
could regain some strength.

When they finally reached Pat's place, Charlie
managed to lap up some water, and nibble feebly at
some cat food. But his eyes were still glazed over, and
he seemed not to know or care who we were. We
worried. Would he be all right? But Charlie remained Charlie, even while he seemed to be breathing his last. As he lay on the floor, totally out of it,
Pat's kitten wandered into the kitchen. Charlie took
one look, staggered to his feet and made a wobbly
dive for the kitten — but Ethel intercepted him and
he promptly collapsed again. We smiled. Charlie was
going to make it!

I carried him into the truck and sped toward for
the vet's office. The doctor confirmed that Charlie
couldn't have lasted much longer. He was running a
fever and thoroughly dehydrated. He had also hurt a
front paw, either when he first ran off or while trying
to find his way out. That was probably why he'd
never made it down the mountain by himself.

Back in the village of Ganges, we stopped to
show Charlie to the Mounties. They seemed as
happy as we were that we'd found him. We also

thanked our friend Anne, as well as the compassionate Mrs. Wooldridge, who had also gone climbing down the mountain to help search.

Lastly, we left a note of gratitude to the Grahams, our absent hosts who had entrusted us with the chalet that provided both their home and their livelihood.

The wonderfully caring people of Salt Spring Island were typical of the Canadians we met all through our motorhome travels. Some day we hope to travel back to Salt Spring — with the dogs on leash.

Times Of The Signs

WHATEVER ELSE HAPPENS as you drive through Alaska, you'll probably become a devout believer in signs — road signs. Otherwise, you might as well be travelling blindfolded in this land where heaving frosts turn the roads into roller coasters, and giant potholes appear overnight. (The pothole is a major industry in the Far North, employing hundreds of construction workers who labor all spring and summer to put the highways back together.) I'm not saying the roads are bad or that you can't get through in decent time, especially on the Alaska Highway. In fact, the roads in Alaska were far better than old-timers had advised us.

The biggest delays we ran into were on the Haines to Haines Junction Highway, where it passes through corners of Canada's British Columbia and Yukon provinces. Even here, the Canadian government had the roads swarming with construction machines. So you'll do fine in your Northern travels except when you hit a bad stretch that hasn't been fixed yet. How bad is bad? The worst.

But you do learn to cope. After a few hundred unpaved miles of RV rock 'n roll, I knew exactly how much to perspire or hyper-ventilate whenever I saw certain signs, such as:

Bumps Roller coaster time. Hit one of these babies too fast, and you'll be floating up against your seat belt like an astronaut. (If you aren't wearing your seat belt, let's hope you come down in the same RV.)

A Black Rectangle With Saw-toothed Top

You're on the jagged edge of trouble if you don't slow down for these patches of rippling, washboard pavement, which could jar the antlers off a bull moose.

Pavement Break The sign you learn to dread the most. It means *no pavement whatsoever.* Just dirt and chunks of stone, and possibly ruts and mudholes as well. The moment you hit a pavement break, your RV becomes an ATV — an all-terrain vehicle — whether you're ready or not. This is where you learn to do the pavement break dance, with an old-fashioned shimmy thrown in.

Construction Next 15 Miles Almost anything could be awaiting you up ahead, except something you want to see. If it's major construction, as it usually is to rate a sign like this, your RV will probably get bounced, jounced and shaken like a paint can in an automatic mixer.

Be Prepared to Stop A sign worth a roll of Rolaids if you're in a hurry. It means there's a flagman just ahead, to warn you of heavy construction machinery or to halt you entirely

while one-lane traffic crawls through behind a
pilot car from the other direction.

The "flagmen" we met were all attractive young
women in work clothes and hard hats. Usually these
flag persons would say something like, "There are
earth-moving trucks ahead. Please give them the
right of way."

Ha! As if those earth-mauling monsters needed
anyone to intercede for them. Like Alaskan grizzlies,
they go where they please. I remember coming
through one massive pavement break where these
multi-tonned earth pushers were roaring back and
forth across the road like overgrown tanks. I waited
for a break in the pattern, floored the accelerator and
just did squeak through as a huge-bladed earth mover
squeezed past us.

Blasting Area   Anyone not paying heed to this
sign could end up in that great RV caravan in the
sky, but no traffic is allowed through when
blasting is actually going on. We encountered this
sign on Alaska's Kenai Peninsula, where road
crews were blasting through solid granite. The
State has spent millions here to improve the
scenic highway to the Kenai, which is Alaska's
playground.

Bad Corner After   seeing   what   pavement
breaks were, I dreaded to find out what Canada
regarded as a "bad corner" on the Haines
Highway. It turned out to be a sharp, steep curve.
I'll admit I was apprehensive as I crept around it,

but there was no one coming the other way. Not a creature was stirring, not even a moose.

Moose Next Seven Miles We saw that road sign right outside of Anchorage, the biggest city in Alaska. And it's no joke. The *Anchorage Times* says that every year several of these enormous animals wander onto the highway and collide with vehicles. It's one thing for hunters to drive home with a moose strapped on their vehicle, but who wants to see one coming through the windshield to land in your lap?

We did see a number of moose and mooselets as we drove along through the wilderness, but didn't actually meet one in the furry flesh until we reached Homer, on the Kenai Peninsula. We were the guests of Beverly Cronen, a California lady who'd just moved up to Alaska and bought a home. We asked how she made her decision.

"There's one reason," she said, pointing out the window at a bull moose that was casually nibbling on her lawn. As the huge beast moved on down her driveway, I asked if this was an unusual occurrence. "Oh, no," she said. "This is his neighborhood. We're the newcomers."

The Alaskan Air Force

WHAT HAS SIX LEGS AND chases moose? The Alaskan mosquito.

No fooling, mosquitoes were chasing moose when we arrived in Alaska. The Anchorage newspaper told of one mighty bull of the woods being stampeded into a river, clear up to his antlers, trying to escape mosquitoes that were using his hide for a blood bank.

Alaskan mosquitoes aren't like the ones we've known in the Lower 48. They are flying hypodermic needles. They're stilettos with wings — live switchblades.

Comparing an ordinary mosquito to one of these ravenous monsters is like comparing a Piper Cub to a Stealth bomber.

The first time I saw one land on the back of my hand, he looked like he'd just flown in off a carrier. I couldn't believe the beak on him. It was big enough to do acupuncture.

We should have suspected what was coming when we checked into the Norlite Campground in Fairbanks. Beside the office was a 10-foot-long metal sculpture of a mosquito, with a plaque identifying it as a member of "The Alaskan Air Force."

We laughed, but soon learned that campgrounds

like this one, filled with juicy tourists, are where Alaskan mosquitoes are most likely to bag their limit in fresh people.

My wife and I were easy prey. The moment we parked our motorhome and ventured outside, a swarm of hungry dive bombers descended upon us. You'd think they had an airfield nearby, with a control tower that sent them over our camp in squadrons.

They roared in low for a frontal assault, going after every inch of exposed skin. Caught off-guard with no repellent on, we danced around from one foot to the other, slapping ourselves silly.

"Back to the motorhome," I shouted. The last time I gave that much blood, I got orange juice and a cookie. Trying to get by without a good repellent during mosquito season makes about as much sense as skinny-dipping in Glacier Bay.

Repellents contain a potent chemical that causes mosquitoes to put on the air brakes in mid-dive, and veer off to spear someone who smells better. But we didn't like the stuff any more than they did.

Our mosquito gunk had a pungent aroma that crinkled our noses, made our eyes squint and numbed our lips. But after we'd been mugged a few times by these Hell's Angels of the insect world, we began thinking of it as perfume.

Once safely back in our motorhome on that first night, I made plans for a defense in depth. I set up a 12-volt bug zapper inside, ready to sizzle any invaders. (It lasted about 10 seconds before shorting out. Maybe the mosquitoes cut the wires.)

Then I got out the repellent and we sloshed it on

to fend off any of those six-legged Draculas who might sneak in. Unfortunately, it was another classic case of underestimating the enemy. We had no idea that an elite force of mosquito commandos had already infiltrated our motorhome when we let the dogs out, and were lying in wait to feast on us.

As we turned out the lights and snuggled down to sleep, the first attack echelon of night fighters came zooming around our ears with an ominous "Zzzzzzzt." I snapped on the lights and grabbed my war club, a rolled-up newspaper.

"Take that!" I cried, splatting them on the windows. I followed this routine several times during the night, hoping to zap them all.

Next morning, Ethel gave me an odd look and said, "Look in the mirror." I did, and saw the mosquitoes had made a landing field of my balding head, the one place I'd forgotten to apply repellent. My scalp looked like a relief map of the moon.

In the days that followed, we fought a running battle with mosquitoes as we journeyed to Denali Park, then Anchorage and on down to Alaska's playground, the Kenai Peninsula. Somehow the mosquitoes managed to stay several bites ahead of us.

If we used repellent, they zapped us in places we missed. If we rubbed it on every exposed place, they still bit right through our clothing, wherever it touched the skin. If we sprayed our clothing, they'd still drill us when the stuff started wearing off. I began wishing I could dive into a pool of repellent and stay under the surface, breathing through a tube.

The biggest assault force yet was waiting to ambush us when a bush pilot dropped us off in the

Kenai wilderness to camp in a meadow not far from the beach. It was worth our lives to go near the beach, even wearing repellent.

As mosquitoes and gnats closed in on us in a grey buzzing cloud, we retreated to get our ultimate defenses — mosquito head nets. Wearing nets kept the mosquitoes off our faces, but it felt like being a prisoner in an onion sack. I kept trying to drink coffee or eat a sandwich through the netting, forgetting that it covered my mouth.

Even our guide, a red-bearded Newfoundlander, was outsmarted by the mosquitoes. He built a fire, boasting that the smoke would keep the little buggers away. But he didn't realize that his shirt was hiking up in the back as he leaned over the fire to cook. Next morning there were several neat rows of bites on his back where the mosquitoes had methodically worked him over, leaving him looking like an advanced case of measles.

Fortunately the mosquito season peaked, and their numbers began to diminish. And there was more good news. We discovered that mosquitoes don't like salt water or windy places. So you can imagine how happy we were to spend a couple of weeks in the mosquito-free paradise of Homer Spit, a fishing village campground where breezes blow most of the time, right off the ocean.

As we headed back down toward the Lower 48, the Anchorage media were reporting that it had been one of the worst mosquito seasons ever. I wasn't surprised, having a knack for being in the right place at the wrong time.

There are Alaskans who will look you right in the eye and say they've seen mosquitoes up there with the wingspan of a bald eagle. Others claim they get as big as Pterodactyls, and carry off wild sheep. But the topper was a bush pilot who swore he barely escaped with his life from a humongous mosquito that chased his helicopter, thinking it was another mosquito of the opposite sex.

Ethel the Adventurer

RVERS ARE MORE adventurous than most folks their age. While others are content to sit home, they are off on the high road, eager to experience what lies ahead. But sometimes adventures can be more than we bargain for — like my wife's climb up a glaciered mountain in Alaska.

While we were staying at Homer Spit Campground, Ethel decided to check out the log cabin office of Katchemak Wilderness Adventures.

"You're in luck," said the smooth-talking proprietor, George Ripley, a legendary outdoorsman who's said to be half grizzly and half mountain goat. George was just putting together a three-day backpacking and river-rafting expedition for the local college. Yes, there was room for Ethel, and at a bargain rate — only $75.

Most of her fellow wilderness trekkers would be hardy Alaskans in their 20s and 30s. Ethel wondered if she could keep up with a super-fit group like that, but George reassured her.

"It'll just be a scamper up some rocks for about five miles," he said. "I've seen you riding your bike around the Spit, and you can handle it."

Ethel pedaled back to our motorhome to sell me

on the trip idea. "You do want to go, don't you?" she asked. "Sure," I lied. "But I can't leave the dogs."

"OK," said she, hiding her disappointment so cleverly that I never did get a glimpse of it. "Mind if I go alone?"

I had misgivings. After all, Ethel was in her 50s, twice the age of those rock-climbing Alaskans. But she really wanted to go, so why not?

George was to lead the "Scamper," aided by a pair of experienced backpackers. They were Tim, a handsome biology student from Middlebury College in Vermont, and Johanna, a free soul in her late 40s who quit a legal secretary's job and sold a comfortable home in Northern California so she could live the outdoor life in the Far North.

What made the expedition all the more tempting was that two of Ethel's new Homer Spit friends would be going along. They were Bev, the adult education planner for the college, and Kimmer, a psychiatric nurse whose father was a famous Alaskan pioneer homesteader. Kimmer brought along her 11-year-old daughter and their pet llama, which had a startling way of demonstrating her affection by sneaking up behind you and breathing in your ear.

On departure morning, I helped lug Ethel's hiking gear down to the dock. Then everyone, including the lovelorn llama, boarded a tiny ferry. The temperature was in the 50s, and the sun was shining as they headed for Harbor Island to begin their adventure.

Now Ethel tells her own story:

When we reached the island, we had to take two

skiffs through the surf. Tim leaped overboard to take
our gear ashore, while George carried us women
piggyback, so we wouldn't have to slosh through the
icy water.

One man in our party was a cancer researcher
from Stanford University who was attired in Eddie
Bauer outdoor togs, and festooned with 35 pounds
of camera gear.

"Is this going to be a canned adventure?" he
asked George.

By that I assumed he meant something as safe
and predictable as a ride in Disneyland. If so, he
lived to eat those words.

Once ashore, we pitched our tents, built a fire of
brush and driftwood, and dined in style on Alaskan
king crab before crawling into our sleeping bags.

Next morning, after a breakfast of fresh-caught
salmon, we started hiking up toward the island's
nearest glacier. As we reached a stream, Bev took off
her jeans and put on jogging shoes to wade across. I
did the same, and it worked fine, as long as you
didn't mind parading around in long johns and
dressing again on the other side.

But there were so many streams to cross that we
finally did it the way a genuine Alaskan does — just
stomp right through the stream, with jeans, boots
and all.

We hiked steadily for several hours, and my
backpack was getting heavier and heavier. I began to
regret every ounce I was overweight, and so did my
knees.

But the rewards were worth it. We topped a rise
at lunch time and saw a spectacular glacial lake, sur-

rounded by a carpet of tundra wild flowers, all deli-
cate blues, pinks and lavenders. You don't see country like *that* in the Lower 48.

After lunch, George suggested diplomatically
that the younger hikers divvy up my backpack, so
I'd have an easier time keeping up.

"We're only as strong as our weakest link," he
said.

Now the path became steeper and so rocky and
slippery that the llama started sliding backward. That
was enough for Kimmer, who decided to turn back
and wait for us at the lake camp below.

George sent our main party on ahead to scout —
and that's the last we ever saw of them until the final
day.

While George made sure that Kimmer and the
llama made it safely down the slope, Bev and I
pushed on. George caught up with us as we skirted
the glacier, climbing higher and higher.

I've never done anything more physically chal-
lenging in my life than scramble up that mountainside, a few feet at a time, looking for handholds and
grabbing at alders that grew on tiny ledges of rock.
There were places so steep that I'd never have made
it if it hadn't been for George, who was always there
to give me a shoulder or knee to brace myself.

Bev, although younger and stronger than I, had
her own problem to deal with — a fear of heights.
She confessed later that she didn't dare look down at
the glacier below, for fear of becoming dizzy and
being unable to continue.

This tortuous climbing went on for hour after
hour. I kept expecting to see the summit at any mo-

ment, but there was always a higher rise just beyond us. George was incredible. He'd carry his backpack to a ridge, then come back for Bev's pack, and help us push on.

As I struggled upward, one handhold at a time, I remembered what my son Steve had said when I asked why he liked rock climbing. "Because you're never so alive as when your life depends on every step you take," he said. I knew now what he meant, for I, too, felt this amazing aliveness, this awareness of every instant.

At last, we reached the top, with its stunning vista of glacier fields and towering ranges extending as far as the eye could see. Back behind us lay the great peninsula of Kenai, with our motorhome camp lost in the distance.

I felt I'd really earned the right to be here. It was wondrous, both intimate and infinite; as close as a tundra flower, and as far as the immense fields of glaciers.

It was literally a "peak" experience, for I felt as if I'd conquered Everest. My left eye was swollen nearly closed by a bug bite, but I couldn't care less. It was so exhilarating to be up there in the sunshine and bracing air, standing on top of the world. That was the high point. The low point still lay ahead.

We hiked on toward our destination, another lake in the distance, but decided to camp for the night when we were unable to catch up with the main group.

George couldn't help noticing my growing difficulties with my knees, so he offered to radio for a 'copter to fly me out if I couldn't keep going. I appreciated the offer, but I wasn't giving up while I still thought I could make it.

The sun was still shining, although it was nearly midnight, when we finally bedded down. We had been climbing, hiking and slogging through rivers for sixteen hours!

We pitched George's tent in an alpine meadow and built a fire of twigs and brush. We feasted on whatever was in the backpacks — instant chicken soup, canned anchovies, dried fruit, crackers and cream cheese.

Next morning, it was time to head down to the river where our rafts were waiting. Swinging a machete, George led us straight through the heavy underbrush, slashing a pathway while striding along so rhythmically and easily that I could barely keep up with him. George, I was discovering, is a man of incredible strength, energy and endurance. If there's one person I'd want to have around in the wilderness, he's the one. (Sorry, Ray!)

Once we made it through the underbrush and rejoined the main group, we saw we'd all have to make our final descent down a steep slope covered with rocks and boulders. One false step and I knew I'd be plunging downward in my own personal avalanche.

While the young men were leaping from boulder to boulder with their 50-pound backpacks, I tried turning around and crawling down backwards to take the pressure off my knees. But it didn't work very well.

Finally I slipped and banged my head. As I started to cry in sheer frustration, a young man saw

my plight and came bounding over to help me all
the way down to the river.

Now we were in for an entirely different adventure, rafting down a swift glacial stream that was
only one degree above freezing. This was great fun,
even though water was sloshing in and soaking our
backpacks. One woman was bounced out into the
water, but she was laughing as she was hauled
aboard, and on we went.

As the waters got rougher, everyone whooped
and hollered while we paddled for dear life to keep
from capsizing. Icy water began flowing right down
the back of my pants. Brrrr!

Once we reached the beach, I sloshed out
through the freezing surf toward the waiting skiff,
carrying my sopping backpack. By now I was too
exhausted to pull myself aboard, so the girl who'd
fallen out of the raft earlier just grabbed and threw
me into the boat, as though she were landing a re-
cord-size halibut.

By the time I made it back to our motorhome, I
looked and felt like a frozen bag lady. Now that it
was over, I realized that:

1. My body wasn't as young and sturdy as it used
    to be.
2. A wilderness trip with real Alaskans is no picnic
    in the park.
3. I'd do it again if I had the chance.

I was proud I'd done it, and all my young companions congratulated me on making it through.
Ray was also proud of me, but said, "Don't you
think you bit off more than you could chew?"
"Yes," I said, "but I did my damndest to chew it."

RV Having Fun Yet?

HAVE YOU EVER HAD THE urge to fly off with a bush pilot for a week of camping in the Alaskan wilderness? It seemed like a wild and crazy idea for a couple of city-bred Californiacs like Ethel and me, but we just couldn't resist it.

George Ripley, a colorful outdoor adventure promoter on Homer Spit, promised it would be "the trip of a lifetime." I didn't stop to consider that the Kenai National Park Wilderness isn't exactly Disney's Adventureland.

George sent along a guide, a portly, red-bearded Canadian named Gordon who could pass for a grizzly. Gordon persuaded us to let him bring along "a great cook." Said cook turned out to be his girlfriend, Pam, a sweet young fish canner. Why we needed a great cook to prepare instant oatmeal is still something of a mystery, especially since we never did catch the alleged cook in the act of cooking anything.

Our expedition got off to a shaky start as we parked our motorhome at the seaplane dock in Homer. I began having second thoughts when I learned why our pilot-to-be, John Berryman of the Beluga Air Service, was several hours late in picking us up. His wife explained he'd gone out on an emergency mission to rescue a party of adventurers much

like ourselves, who had been stranded without food
or water in bear country.

It was nearly 10 P.M., but still daylight when John
finally returned with his four-passenger Beaver prop
plane and the people he'd rescued. We had enough
gear waiting on the dock to outfit a Polar expedition:
two folding kayaks, two tents, sleeping bags, air mattresses, fishing gear and enough food for eight days,
in case we got socked in by bad weather.

Ethel climbed aboard with our guide and the alleged cook. Then I handed our dogs across to the pilot, who stood on one pontoon and hoisted them up
to Ethel.

As the heavily laden plane labored slowly down
the bay for takeoff, Ethel and I sat squeezed beneath
50 pounds of dog apiece in our laps, laughing at the
absurdity of it all.

I wondered if our Beaver would ever rise from its
pond, but it was soon climbing rapidly, circling back
over Homer Spit and then heading across the ice
fields of Kenai Peninsula. We soared past one glacier
after another, over pristine mountain lakes and meadows, finally crossing the 5,000-foot snowy peaks to
the ocean.

We cruised in and out of several wilderness fjords,
looking for a place to set down. The pilot explained
that he had to find a spot that was sufficiently pro-
tected from the open sea, so that he could safely
come back for us.

Our original choice for a landing, Surprise Bay,
was indeed a surprise because somebody was already
tenting there. We cruised onward, buzzing several
other strips of beach before finally choosing Quartz

Bay, in the western arm of the Kenai Fjord. It was a rocky but sheltered stretch of shoreline, ideal for camping. John brought the Beaver down onto the bay and taxied close to shore.

We crawled out and waded through the icy water with the dogs and all our gear, ready to play Swiss Family Robinson. An armada of mosquitoes rose up to greet us, but we were ready for them. We broke out our head nets and sloshed our "Jungle Juice" repellent all over our bodies, forcing the mosquitoes to back off.

Up from the beach lay a tundra meadow. After clearing the area of rocks and stumps, we set up our geodesic tent, a modern marvel of high-tech simplicity. I have a long and melancholy history of wrestling with tent poles that crash down on me like the pillars that clobbered Samson. But this tent was so easy to figure out that I put it up all by myself.

The weather held just long enough for us to set up camp and unroll our mattresses. Then we snuggled in, dogs and all, for a night of sleep in dry comfort while the rains fell without letup.

It was still too stormy the next morning to do much. Gordon fixed breakfast in the rain while the alleged cook was getting her beauty sleep. Gordon served us instant oatmeal, Tang, tea and coffee. The drinks were made with water from a nearby waterfall, sterilized with halozone tablets.

Unsinkable Ethel was eager to go kayaking, so the moment the weather cleared that afternoon, Gordon and I assembled the sturdy kayaks, called Folbots. They were easily put together with numbered wooden pieces and color-coded aluminum poles.

Gordon said they're very stable afloat, because you sit below water level.

(You don't want to tip over in Alaskan waters because you'd freeze in minutes like a supermarket salmon.)

Soon Ethel and I were out in the bay in our very own kayak, paddling in unison like a team of old wilderness types. It was a thrill to be moving smoothly through the water with rhythmic strokes of the double-bladed oars. I kept the beat going by singing *Sixteen Men on a Dead Man's Chest*. (Okay, so the Eskimos don't do that. But I don't know any Eskimo sea chanteys.)

We paddled a quarter-mile to the foot of a steep waterfall where we could see a dozen salmon trying to leap across a rocky barrier into a pool to spawn. St. Ethel of Assisi took pity on one 8-pounder that couldn't make it, caught it with her bare hands and gently released it in the pool.

Meanwhile, we had left the dogs in camp. We weren't worried about them because the beach was hemmed in by steep cliffs, so we figured they couldn't get lost or into trouble. But when we returned, we discovered that the mosquitoes had all but flown off with poor Charles and Lena, biting their exposed undersides in dozens of places. From then on, we sprayed the dogs as well as ourselves.

The next day's weather was truly terrible, with hour after hour of steady rain. We huddled inside our tent in the final stages of claustrophobia, but grateful that the tent remained dry inside. To be wet inside and out, with no change of clothes, is a camper's nightmare.

As the rains pelted the tent, the dogs licked their mosquito-reddened tummies and looked at us with sorrowful, accusing eyes. Charles was dripping and bedraggled after having to venture out on nature's call. He was also uncharacteristically mulish, shoving his way into the middle of the tent to stake out more room.

I could almost read his thoughts: "What are we doing here, jammed into this tiny, damp space, surrounded by falling water?"

Ethel and I passed the time reading paperbacks. After hours of the most rain we'd ever seen, I began hoping that George, the promoter who sold us on this "adventure," was also out somewhere in the wilderness, sopping wet and utterly miserable.

By morning the storm had pushed on, and the weather was glorious. The dogs romped like puppies in the sunshine. We dragged out all our damp clothes and sleeping bags, and spread them atop the tents to dry. Then we had more instant hot cereal a la halozone.

Gordon had a kayaking trip already charted that would take us into a neighboring fjord, via a stretch of open sea. However, I wasn't exactly keening to paddle a kayak through ocean swells. What would we do if it suddenly sprang a leak, or overturned?

"Stay with the kayak until Pam and I can paddle alongside," Gordon said. "We'll lay a pair of oars across from boat to boat as handholds. Then you take turns coming up between the oars to hoist yourself into our boat, while we lean to the far side to keep balance."

Easy for him to say. I pictured Ethel and me

floundering about in the icy water, gasping in shock while trying to climb into Gordon's kayak before we froze to death. Even if we made it aboard, we'd be blue-faced, teeth-chattering nervous wrecks.

And then what? "Then," said Gordon, "Pam and I would bail out your boat." "With what?" He pointed to a pair of cook pots he had stashed in the bow. "With those." He didn't say what would happen if *his* boat capsized.

The weather was sunny again as we boarded our kayak and paddled round the point of our fjord into open water, bobbing easily on the swells. I gained confidence as we zigzagged through a small cluster of islands, then paddled into the safety of the next fjord, exploring for a place to fix lunch.

We found a beach with its own running stream, where more salmon were trying to wriggle up the rocks. Ethel took pity on another salmon that wasn't making the ascent, and carried it back to the ocean. I doubt the expectant salmon appreciated this, but Ethel felt better.

We started a fire on our portable cook stove and had lunch. Then we paddled back through rolling ocean swells to our own cove again, feeling rather proud of ourselves. That evening we sat around a beach campfire, roasting hot dogs and marshmallows. It had been a perfect day, with the sun shining until well after bedtime.

We made optimistic plans for more kayaking and some fishing, but the next day was the pits. We awoke to the drumming of an even bigger downpour that before, one that never let up for 16 hours straight. The dogs had to be pushed bodily outside to do their business.

Gordon and the alleged cook had left camp at 3 a.m. when the weather was still fine, to get in a kayaking trip of their own. But as the big storm moved in, with great gusts of wind clawing at our tent, we started to worry. Unless they were lucky enough to put in somewhere for shelter, they had to be paddling for their lives out there in the open ocean. By late afternoon they were hours overdue. How could they survive, we wondered, if they capsized in those pounding seas, with no help anywhere near?

Paddle or Perish

WHEN OUR GUIDE AND THE
alleged cook finally did straggle into camp with a tale
of near-disaster at sea, they were sopping wet and
chilled to the marrow. Gordon's hands and face were
the color of halibut. Pam was utterly spent, hardly
able to stand up.

They'd had a very scary voyage, paddling against
rising winds through heavy swells while freezing sea
water dripped down inside their parka sleeves with
every stroke of the oars. They nearly drowned when
they made the mistake of seeking shelter inside a sea
cave. Heavy swells thundered in upon their kayak,
slamming them up against the rocky walls and nearly
swamping their battered craft. They fought for their
lives, struggling with all the strength they could sum-
mon up to turn the kayak around, until at last they
could paddle back into the open sea.

The ordeal left Pam too exhausted to talk. She
huddled in a blanket inside her tent, shivering vio-
lently. Gordon brought the cookstove inside so they
could both thaw out. Then they went straight to bed.

Gordon confided later that he had persuaded Pam
to share his sleeping bag, telling her that this was a
survival technique to warm chilled bodies. He said
they slept in the buff, wrapped in each other's arms. I

could only admire Gordon's selfless gesture.

Next day the sun came out, and just in time, because our tent and everything in it was wet from condensation. We gathered up all our sodden garments and stretched them out to dry on a huge tree trunk that had washed ashore during the storm.

Afternoon was play time. Ethel and Pam went kayaking together, sticking close to camp in sheltered waters. Gordon and I paddled out in hopes of a fish dinner, but the fish just weren't biting after the storm.

Since we couldn't get a nibble with rod and reel, we headed for a waterfall where we'd seen salmon leaping, and netted a superb pair of kings for dinner. We feasted on the beach that evening, baking the salmon in the coals of our campfire and toasting marshmallows for dessert.

The next morning was to be getaway day, but our beach was socked in again by low-scudding clouds that drenched us with heavy rain. We started packing nevertheless, on the chance that our bush pilot would somehow break through the weather to pick us up.

We left the tents standing until last because they were our only shelter from the downpour. Meanwhile, both dogs were wringing wet again.

As we finished our chores, we heard the muffled throbbing of a prop engine somewhere above the clouds. Like the little fellow in the old *Fantasy Island* TV series, I ran out of our tent yelling, "The plane! The plane!"

Gordon stuck his head out, smiling in relief. But then the sound faded away, and so did Gordon's smile as we all ducked back inside our tents.

Ten minutes later, we heard a plane approaching again. This time it dropped right down through a momentary break in the rainclouds, and we saw that it was our winged ark, pilot John Berryman's blue and white Beaver pontoon craft.

John taxied close to shore. He climbed out wearing hip boots, and jumped into the water to brace his plane against the tidal surges while we struck the tents and scurried back and forth in frantic haste with all our bags of gear.

Then we shoehorned ourselves and the dogs back on board the plane. Berryman taxied into the middle of the fjord, turned into the wind, slammed the throttle and sent us climbing upward. Meanwhile, the weather had worsened, shutting down the mountain pass that John had just flown through to reach us. He changed course for a longer but safer journey through another pass where visibility was better. He didn't charge us extra for the longer flight, however. Bush pilots are like that. A deal is a deal.

After landing at the seaplane dock, we loaded our gear into the RV and headed back toward Homer Spit campground.

Compared to our tent in the wilderness, the RV seemed like a four-star hotel. We luxuriated in hot water, hot food, dry comfy beds, space to move around, and a TV set to put us back in touch with the nonsense called civilization.

Our week in the wilderness could have been the vacation of a lifetime if only Mother Nature had cooperated. Even so, it was wonderful, it was miserable, it was unforgettable adventure in the raw. As another RVer put it, "After Alaska, everywhere else is Kansas."

Checklist for Survival

AFTER A YEAR OF STEADY motorhoming, I developed a handy little list of do's and don'ts for how to survive and enjoy yourself while traveling in an RV.

Any expert will tell you the common sense things, like using a checklist so you won't drive off with your power cord following you umbilically down the highway. But you have to roll up a few thousand miles on your own to learn the things that the experts *don't* tell you.

Take that checklist, for example. My first item isn't even mentioned by experts, but I can't over-emphasize its importance:

Make sure your mate is aboard.

Wives and husbands have been left like so many stray cats all up and down our interstates. This has resulted in what are euphemistically known as "strains in the relationship."

One RVer said he wasn't aware that he'd left his wife in a gas station phone booth until a patrol car with his abandoned spouse in the back seat pulled him over. "She's kinda quiet," he explained.

Here's another biggie that the experts never mention:

Check to see there is no one in the commode before you

go over a speed bump.

If you forget, you will probably hear a shriek, followed by a blistering stream of colorful language. If you've been going too fast, the commodist may even have to be extricated from the shower after re-entry. To avoid this happening in your RV, I suggest you put up a sign banning commodery in transit, or install a seat belt.

Next item: *Be sure the refrigerator is locked.*

Our carpet has already had three milk baths. Walk barefoot on it, and your toes churn butter. (I heard of a fellow who forgot to lock his party coach refrigerator as he drove off one morning, after an evening of high-test frivolity. Out spilled an entire pitcher of Margaritas. He says his dog helped him clean up, but couldn't bark straight for days.)

Another suggestion:

Make sure your gray-water tank isn't full before taking a shower.

Otherwise, you may find yourself showering from the bottom up, so to speak. Water spurting up from the drain, artesian style, can be a real problem, especially if your feet and ankles are not dishwasher-safe.

Never store heavy objects in upper cabinets.

I used to keep large boxes of music cassettes in our overhead cabinets until the day they all came cascading down upon our terrified young Doberman. To this day, she casts a nervous glance to heaven as she sneaks past the cabinet to her nest under the passenger's dashboard, where she is safe from UFO's.

Before selecting a space at an RV park, drive through and check what's going on.

This is how you can avoid finding yourself parked

next to people who play hard rock tunes with all the windows open, through speakers better suited for SWAT teams. I always keep an eye out for some kindly looking guy who's puttering around outside his rig with his toolbox. I just sleep better knowing there's a tinkerer around who can fix things that go kaflooey in the middle of the night.

(I remember waking up during the pre-dawn hours in a Canadian RV park, and listening drowsily to a babbling brook. Then I realized we hadn't parked anywhere *near* a brook. Our water hose had blown its outside connection and was turning the park into a lake.)

Here are some practical tips on RV driving:

Drivers of larger RVs should be especially careful about hitting small cars.

Small cars are not only harder to see, but after you hit them, they tend to collect under your bumper. Nothing can reduce your mileage like an impacted Hyundai.

If you are about to collide with an old clunker, swing your RV toward the nearest expensive car instead.

(He's the one with insurance.)

If an accident is not your fault, yell, "Police!" If it is your fault, yell, "Whiplash!"

Offer the other driver a good stiff drink to relax, but don't have one yourself until after the police have run tests on you both with their breathalyzers.

Home is Where You Park It

RVERS SEEM TO BE AMONG the happiest folks in the USA. Retirees in particular. We kept meeting relaxed and carefree senior citizens who confessed to but one real regret — that they didn't retire earlier.

Besides traveling just for the fun of it, many seniors take advantage of their RVs as we did, to check out potential places to retire or use as a home base when they're not on the road.

It would have been simpler for us to keep our home in Los Angeles, but the city has become so choked by traffic that you can gnash your teeth down to the gums just getting across town.

Ethel and I finally got fed up with sitting in bumper to bumper traffic for hours at a time, especially in our own driveway. We decided it was time to find a saner existence.

Our first choice was still somewhere in California, if we could find reasonable housing in a smaller town. Besides the mild climate, we've always enjoyed the Granola State and all its flakes.

(Whether you're a Baptist, a Buddhist, a speaker in tongues or a gong-banging guru lover, California is the place to find folks who share your enthusiasms.)

California is no longer a paradise of sandaled seers,

orange groves and sleepy pueblos. It's more like a nation in itself, home to some 30 million over-enlightened souls.

We started looking in Northern California's wine region, and we certainly weren't disappointed by the countryside. The wine country is as lush (no pun intended) as ever. Its vineyards act as greenbelts, separating its little agricultural towns so they don't all slurb together like all those once-separate communities in Southern California.

(Few Southern Californians really seem to know or care where one city leaves off and another begins. The best way to tell is by reading the lettering on the side of the police car when you get a ticket.)

We loved Napa and Sonoma counties, but we'd arrived in the midst of a heat wave. Hot weather's fine if you're a grape, but we were wilting like ferns in a sauna.

And so we drank farewell to grapeland, and headed for Capitola, a popular sand and surf town just south of Santa Cruz. San Franciscans like going to Capitola because it's usually free of fog, even when other coastal areas are socked in.

We arrived during spring break. The town was awash in high school and college kids, all having a terrific time.

Several beauties were wearing swimsuits cut so high in the rear that they made bikinis look like Mother Hubbards. (I hadn't seen so much bared flesh since my newspaper days, when I covered, if that's the word, a nudist colony picnic gathering. You should have seen those nudies playing volleyball.)

Lost in nostalgia for the girls of my own youth, I

drove slowly down the main street, watching the nu-
bile parade until Ethel muttered, "Eyes on the road,
you old rake." She always gets perturbed when I start
driving up onto sidewalks.

"How about living here?" I asked. She shook her
head. "Too crowded." Of course it's too crowded," I
said. "It's Easter week." But she was not to be dis-
suaded by a mere fact, so off we went.

San Diego was another possible place to anchor
our lives, for we remembered it as a quiet village that
nodded off whenever the Navy shipped out to sea.
But San Diego slumbers no more. Now the second-
largest city in California, its suburbs have grown like
bamboo in Bangkok. As we drove through north San
Diego County, we saw one huge new housing tract
after another, stretching to the horizon.

All this massive construction lay within a gas cap's
throw of the San Diego Freeway, already one of the
busiest and slowest in Southern California. If the
population here keeps growing, California may yet
witness an automotive apocalypse, one giant gridlock
from border to border.

When we told friends of our search for a new
home base, a friend with a condo in Palm Springs invited us to sample the desert scene. It was well above
100 degrees when we arrived, but we seemed to be
the only ones who noticed the heat. The tennis
courts were filled with hatless maniacs who were
whomping the ball and racing about as if it were
spring at Wimbledon.

Ethel and I fled to the pool, but the water felt as if
they'd set the thermostat at slow simmer. To survive
the midday sun, I had to stay in the pool in a safari

hat and wet T-shirt, or plunge back in every few minutes when the shirt dried out. It was *that hot*.

"Isn't this great?" asked my buddy, Bruce Howard, as he walked off the tennis court. He was dripping like a cheap faucet.

"Yeah, terrific!" I said, while pressing my back against the patio wall to enjoy half an inch of noon-day shade. I couldn't wait to get back into our RV, even though it was hot enough to pop toast, so we could escape from Bruce's beloved desert.

Another friend from Snohomish, Washington, invited us to come see the forest and mountain vistas of the Northwest. The scenery was dazzling. It was also drizzling.

We were marooned in an RV park outside Seattle by a downpour that lasted for two straight weeks. I started wondering when a dove would show up with an olive twig. Seattle deserves its ranking as one of the most beautiful and interesting cities anywhere, but it's no haven for sun lovers.

As our search went on, we realized there was a "good, but" qualifier to go with every place we visited. Palm Springs was wonderful in the winter, but . . . Seattle was fantastic in the summer, but . . . So we decided to head inland and explore the towns of the Great Southwest — Arizona, Utah, New Mexico and Colorado.

Here Come the Brides

BACK IN THE 1870S, federal marshals were hunting down Mormons hiding in Utah to escape prosecution for polygamy. On a sweep through the town of Lehi, one marshal asked a young boy if he could point out any polygamists. "Sure," said the boy. He led the Feds into the family barnyard and pointed to their rooster.

I was reminded of this story when Ethel and I went cruising through Utah as part of our ongoing search for a permanent home base.

We wanted to see the town of St. George, a pleasant and relaxed little community of about 12,000. Some experts rank St. George as one of the top retirement places in the country. It lies in the scenic red sandstone country of Utah's southern Dixie region, where semi-tropical temperatures prevail during the long summer, and the climate is warm in winter.

Pioneer church leader Brigham Young, who founded the Mormon Temple in Salt Lake City, had a winter home in St. George. He organized the great Mormon trek from the Mississippi Valley across the plains, mountains and arid desert to Utah in the 1840s.

Young preached polygamy, and he practiced what

he preached, taking 17 wives and siring 57 children. In the wake of the federal prosecutions, the church itself banned polygamy in 1890.

After visiting the Young home, we became curious about a beautifully restored, three-story Victorian bed-and-breakfast across the way with the intriguing name of Seven Brides.

The owner was a great-granddaughter of Ben Johnson, a Mormon pioneer who did indeed have seven brides — and 45 children. Although that number of progeny won't get him into any *Guinness Book of Records,* he certainly led a blessed eventful life. The pitter-patter of tiny feet around his house must have been deafening.

I don't know for sure, but I would imagine that those early Mormon settlers wed their wives one at a time, much as an athlete gradually adds more weights to his barbell.

Nevertheless, I can't help visualizing what a mass wedding for seven brides might be like:

The groom, Obediah Wilkins, limps to the altar, favoring the sore knees he suffered while doing all that proposing. The soloist sings seven choruses of *Oh Promise Me,* and seven proud fathers march their daughters down the aisle to seven renditions of *Here Comes The Bride.*

The pastor struggles through a wall-to-wall crush of bridesmaids and matrons to reach the altar and begin the ceremony, which climaxes like this:

"Do you, Obediah Wilkins, take Rebecca, Rachel, Sarah, Clara, Faith, Hope and Charity to be your wedded wives?"

The groom nods and says, "I do-do-do-do-do-

do-do." Then he places seven rings on seven fingers, and kisses his way down the bridal line with a tender impartiality.

Seven bridal bouquets go sailing through the air, and the brides board seven waiting wagons. The honeymoon wagon train ends up at a rural hideaway just for eight. Then the groom carries all his brides over the threshold. (Or maybe he doesn't. Who needs an aching back on top of sore knees when facing a seven inning honeymoon?)

It's probably just as well that polygamy was outlawed, because modern life in the USA is complicated enough without all that spousing around. If Obediah were alive today, I'd bet my last silver dollar that he'd get nailed for an audit by the Internal Revenue Service

I can just see the IRS agent leafing through Obediah's return, saying, "Mr. Wilkins, there must be some mistake here. You are claiming 58 exemptions."

"That's right," says Obediah, "eight for me and the missuses, and 50 for the kids."

"You have seven wives and 50 children?"

Obediah smiles shyly. "So far."

"It says here, Mr. Wilkins, that you made $40,000 last year. That's a lot of money for a man with only two acres of turnips."

"Not really," says Obediah. "My wives made that money workin' in Wilkinsville. I didn't even pick them turnips 'cause of my back."

"You claim a $150,000 deduction for child care. Isn't that a little high?"

"Nope," says Obediah. "What with the wives

workin' and me laid up with a screamin' sacroiliac, we had to hire the entire Wilkinsville Ladies Auxiliary to look after the kids."

The interview ends as Obediah walks out with a $1,000 refund, which he spends at the nearest kiddies' shoe store.

And what if a modern Obediah took his family motorhoming? As he stops his caravan at an RV park for the night, he asks the manager, "Any spaces left?"

"Sure. We've got half a dozen."

"I'll take 'em," says Obediah.

"All of them?"

"Yep," says Obediah. "The wives git real fussy unless they have their own beds, so I travel with three motorhomes, two kiddie cabooses that sleep the 50 young'ns, and a chuck wagon."

"I see," says the manager. "And where do *you* sleep?"

"In the chuck wagon. Man's gotta have his rest."

There may still be some modern Obediahs, part of a breakaway group reportedly still practicing polygamy in a remote region of Arizona. I have no wish to join them. But sometimes, married as I am to the ever-changing Ethel, I feel I already have several wives. However, that's OK. It's been great fun living with all of them.

Rocky Mountain High

I'D MUCH RATHER SEE A level stretch of highway ahead than a range of mountains, no matter how beautiful they are. Ever since we came rocketing down the Donner Pass on our very first motorhome adventure, brakes smoking like a blaze in a tire factory, the mere thought of mountain driving shifts my pulse into overdrive.

Remembering that wild ride, I could feel the adrenaline pumping again as we headed up into the Rocky Mountains on our latest safari to find a new home base. And it wasn't just the driving from southern Utah up into the high country of Colorado that was giving me pause. I kept wondering how our sealevel lungs would react to breathing air thin enough to make a carburetor cough.

It was a fairly gradual climb from 2800-foot St. George, Utah, through the scenic sandstone buttes and gorges of Zion National Park, and then into the high desert sagebrush and red rock country of Northern Arizona. By nightfall, we'd crossed the Colorado border into Cortez, a cattle and commercial center. This area is known as the Four Corners, the one place in the United States where the borders of four states meet.

Next morning, an hour up the road, we reached

the town we wanted most to see, Durango. We'd read in various retirement books that Durango was one of the top 10 places in America. Tourists come to this region to enjoy every outdoor sport imaginable, from hiking, fishing and river-rafting to some of the finest skiing in the country.

Durango even has its own unique tourist attraction, the famous Durango & Silverton Narrow Gauge Railroad. A coal-burning steam engine, pulling wooden coaches and open gondolas of the 1880s, puffs its way up through the pine-forested San Juan Mountains. The tracks lead to the old mining town of Silverton, 45 miles away, at an altitude of 9000 feet.

We joined the train riders and had a great time chugging through the wilderness, which hasn't changed since miners rode these same rails to reach Silverton's gold and silver mines a century ago. Then we wandered and browsed around Silverton, which friends described as "a ghost town that refuses to die." Life was certainly lively enough at the ornately Victorian Grand Imperial Hotel where tourists were enjoying lunch. The hotel is now fully restored to its original splendor, with decorative tin ceilings and Gay Nineties decor.

Returning to Durango, we began checking out what life could be like in this handsome town with its restored Victorian buildings that look much the same as they did a century ago. We were pleased to learn that Durango's housing prices were still moderate. One major reason for this, however, has been that there weren't many jobs available for newcomers. So while Durango is fine for retirees with their own sources of income, it's more difficult for active working people to relocate there.

Just how attractive is Durango? Consider this: Although it has only 13,470 residents, they include a hundred physicians, surgeons, and psychotherapists, and fifty dentists. There is a modern, well equipped hospital as well, serving 35,572 residents throughout La Plata County. All this at a time when many other small towns are begging for medical professionals. A young attorney told me, "You have to forget about making lots of money if you want to live here, but the quality of life is what we value the most."

Durango, altitude 6,512 feet, really is a pretty little place. It's on the banks of the Animas River and is surrounded by spectacular snow-capped peaks. Since the town is just 20 miles north of the New Mexico border, in Southwest Colorado's "banana belt," its four season climate is considered fairly mild.

Springtime, with its wildflower vistas, fresh breezes and brilliant skies was a heady experience for us smogified, traffic-numbed refugees from the megalopolis.

But since we were unaccustomed to the thinner air, we did our share of gasping for breath like fresh-netted trout the first few days. We napped a lot, too. But that occasional feeling of breathlessness started to go away after a few more days. By the time we headed back for Los Angeles, we felt fairly normal.

(I'd been told that adjusting to higher altitudes involves producing more hemoglobin to increase the blood's capacity to carry oxygen. So I presumed that if we did live in the Rockies, our hemoglobin and shemoglobin would soon wise up and start multiplying.)

Meanwhile, Ethel and I agreed that Durango had the most appeal as a future home of any place we'd seen. We decided to settle in and rent a while to make sure that this little paradise was really what it seemed.

Have an Icy Day

THE BIGGEST SNOWSTORM of the year was blanketing the high country of Southwest Colorado, and the road was icier than a polar bear's backside. I was having second thoughts about the wisdom of being out here in such weather, even in a car with four-wheel drive.

That's when I saw what looked like a motorhome looming up behind me out of the swirling whiteness. Impossible, I thought. Not out here, where cars were sliding sideways on black ice.

Just minutes before, climbing the last grade, I'd passed a tractor-trailer that had lost traction and slid backwards, right to the edge of a drop-off. I would have turned back right then, but visiting relatives were due to arrive at the local airport, and I had to pick them up.

Now, just ahead, there was more trouble. A huge blue trash truck had slid off into the ditch. Traffic was blocked in both directions while a pair of heavy duty tow trucks winched away at cables, straining to haul it back out onto the road.

As traffic waited, I wondered what a motorhome was doing out here in the midst of this big storm. Why wasn't the man at the wheel taking it easy somewhere in Florida or Arizona, working on his tan? He was either the greatest driver since Barney Oldfield, or the wildest since Mr. Toad.

I bundled up and got out to wave at the motor-homer. He and his wife both waved back as if they hadn't a care in the world, even though their rig was festooned from bumper to bumper with huge icicles. I was dying to ask them what they were doing, but traffic started moving again, and I had to run back to my car.

Now I think I've solved the mystery. They must have been skiers. I say this because I spotted half a dozen more motorhomes the next day at Purgatory-Durango Ski Resort, just up the mountain from Durango. They were parked in a special area for RVers who were taking advantage of the best skiing of the season.

One of these RV ski buffs, Clarence Melancon of Spring, Texas, set me straight about driving a motor-home in wintry conditions. He and his wife, Irene, have a 27-footer with steel-belted radials. He said it handles just fine on snowy roads. "I used to live in Chicago," he said, "and a lot of us preferred steel-belted radials over snow tires."

He said he was planning to camp in style next season at Hermosa Meadows, just 15 miles from Pur-gatory. Campground Owner Glenn Francis told me he hosts dozens of RV skiers every winter. Some carry chains, but they aren't usually needed except at certain times in the high passes.

"We get a lot of families coming back year after year," Francis said. "It's much cheaper for them than renting motels or condos — and more convenient, too."

Hermosa Meadows has 20 winterized full-hookup sites equipped with heat tapes to keep both pipes and outside tank valves from freezing, and 20 other sites with electricity only. Some RVers leave their rigs there all season, so they can ski whenever they wish. Cottonwood, another all-season campground, is in Durango, half an hour from the ski slopes.

After meeting these skiers, I realized I've been missing something. All my life I'd avoided downhill skiing for fear of breaking a couple of clavicles, or swallowing a ski pole, and thereby missing a day's work.

On the other hand, my new friends in Durango now included both a veteran ski instructor and a paramedic, so I figured I was set.

There was just one catch: Could the instructors really turn a guy my age into a snow bunny? I needn't have worried.

When those instructors say they take skiers of all ages, they mean it. Here I was, in my early 60s, feeling pretty macho to be taking a lesson; but my teacher, an attractive young lady named Sandy, made me feel like a kid when she told me of a Texan she had taught the previous season.

"He was 95 years old," Sandy said. "He came up with his children, grandchildren and great-grandchildren, and they all took lessons."

"Weren't you a little worried he might keel over on you?"

"Well, yes," she said. "So at lunchtime, I studied a booklet on CPR."

But the old codger made it, hanging in there all week for five straight lessons until he could swing on down the slopes with all his progeny.

Ninety-five is a rather unusual age at which to be skiing, or even breathing, but Sandy assured me it's not at all rare for seniors in their 70s and even 80s to take up the sport.

So, I signed up. The hardest thing about skiing, I soon learned, is walking in ski boots. They clamp onto your ankles like a demented bulldog and make you walk like Frankenstein.

My first lesson went fairly well, except that I flunked ski lift. The lift chair sneaked up from behind and scooped me up with a thump so hard that I yelped in surprise. (Now I know how the Swiss invented yodeling.)

Then the chair dumped me off at the top of the ski run in a humiliating sprawl, directly in the path of other skiers who dodged while I scrambled on all fours to get out of their way. By lesson's end, however, I could stay upright for several seconds at a time. I could even snowplow, if you count sliding backward.

Two seasons later, I was still taking lessons, but confident enough to go bopping down the slopes like all the college kids on winter break, along with the teen-age "shred heads" who zoom by on snowboards.

I even met a local doctor, a retiree in his late 60s, who still skiis even though both his hips are artificial. "Hey," he said, "It's my life and this is how I want to live it."

Up, Up and Away

SOME DAY SOON A motorhome could be put into orbit, powered by an energy beam from Earth. And if the RVers aboard wanted to visit Mars in their rover vehicle, they could — fueled by energy from an orbiting power station.

Now, hold it. You're thinking that I've finally snapped my wig, right? That the old brain is a quart low, and the rubber isn't meeting the road.

Well, listen to this: According to the *New York Times*, researchers at Rensselaer Polytechnic Institute (RPI) have already been designing a small beam powered spaceship that could rapidly carry five people into Earth orbit.

"It's easy because there's no fuel," *The Times* was told by Leik N. Myrabo, an engineering physicist at RPI.

"The vehicle weighs six tons, about the same as a 35-foot Winnebago. You could throw in the family dog and be orbiting in three to four minutes."

OK, so the man said a spaceship the *size* of a Winnebago. Picky, picky. The point is, we will be able to put an RV in orbit if we want to.

As *The Times* explained, beaming energy is like radio broadcasting, but at higher levels. The flying

machine, equipped with a special antenna on its underside, picks up the microwaves from a ground station and turns them into electrical power.

Beam energy is far more efficient than current space shuttle technology. At liftoff, regular fuel for the shuttle's main engines and booster rockets makes up about 85 per cent of its total weight. If the shuttle could get its energy via a microwave beam, its payload capacity would increase from 30 tons to nearly 2000 tons.

What does this all mean to RVers? Well, we're an adventurous lot. As soon as those five passenger Winnebagish things start zipping off into orbit, somebody's going to want to go RVing in space.

I'm no technical expert, but I think it's safe to assume the average motorhome will need a few changes before launching. More weatherstripping, for example, so the oxygen doesn't leak out before you can make it to the next dealer satellite. You might also need a bigger radiator to handle the extra heat from atmospheric friction during re-entry. But once your machine was certified spaceworthy, you'd be up, up and away.

Since beaming energy to space craft is already in the planning stages, let's peek ahead to RVing in the future. It is now the 21st Century, and the hottest sellers on any RV dealer's lot are those new Interplanetary Recreation Vehicles, known as IRVs.

After reading the latest ads in Orbit Home magazine, RVer Max Power and his wife, Dyna, go shopping for their first space coach. They visit Spaceland IRV Center, where several different makes are on display.

They wander around the lot, dazzled by luxurious new flying machines such as the Starabago, the Space Arrow, the Jetstream, Holiday Lunar Rambler, the Spacey Daze Moonrader and Xplorer Orbiteer.

As Max is kicking the landing tires of the latest Starabago, a salesman approaches with a smile like the man in the moon.

"Help you folks?"

Max asks how much power it has, since getting into orbit is pretty much uphill, so to speak.

"Power?" says the salesman. "You could fly this thing to the sun! In fact, I'm going there in one of these babies with the boss next month."

Max looks puzzled, saying, "I don't think you should try that. If you get anywhere near the sun, your ship would be vaporized by the heat."

The salesman gives him a condescending look. "Don't worry, Mr. Power, we thought of that. We're not gonna go in the daytime."

Dyna wants to know if the Starabago can accommodate pets.

"Glad you asked," says the salesman, leading them inside to a sealed Petarium with feeding ports.

"This here is all pressurized and temperature controlled," says the salesman. "You got your miniaturized fire hydrant right there to make a space dog feel at home, and there's even a solar-powered sandbox for your cat.'

"What about television?," asks Dyna. "When we're in orbit, can I still watch 'Oprah Winfrey'?"

"You can do better than that," says the salesman. "You'll be orbiting right next to the broadcasting satellites, so all you gotta do is run a cable to the nearest one, and bingo! You're watchin' HBO movies, and it won't cost you nothin'.''

Max is fascinated by the Space Potty, an elaborate-looking gadget that is something like a cross between a holding tank and a vacuum cleaner.

"The Space Potty hooks right into your spacesuit with a hose," the salesman says, "so you don't have to take your suit off any more to, ah, go. It's even got a reverse switch for easy cleaning, but you wanna keep it on safety so's it won't accidentally back up on you while you're still wearing it."

"What if it did?"

"You wouldn't wanna know."

Max and Dyna are so impressed that Max writes out a check for a million bucks right then and there. (Fortunately, inflation in the 21st century has raised Max's salary as a rocket bus driver to $2 million a year.)

That night they're deciding where to go.

" I'd love to visit the moon," says Dyna.

"Yeah," says Max, "but I'm not drivin' you over it. I've seen the lunar postcards, and that moon's got more potholes than Jersey City."

"How about Mars?" says his wife. "We could see the canals, maybe go for a ride in a Martian gondola."

"Not on our first trip," says Max. "I don't want to be more than half a million miles from a dealer, in case that Space Potty gives us trouble."

So they compromise on a shakedown trip to Walt's RV Park, which is in stationary orbit over Disneyland.

"Look what this puppy can do," says Max,

tromping down on the beam accelerator.

"Careful," says Dyna. "You're goin' pretty fast."

"We're in outer space, for gosh sakes," says Max. "Where can'tcha go fast?"

His wife's reply is drowned out by the sound of a siren. Max looks out the porthole and sees a Skyway Patrolman on a lunar cycle.

"What did I tell you?," says Dyna. "He must've been hiding behind that last asteroid."

"Don't worry," says Max. "I'll tell him it's our first trip, and he'll probably let me off with a warning."

"But what if he gives you a ticket?"

Max gets a fiendish grin as he says, "Then I'll invite him in to use the Space Potty."

Let the Good Times Roll

T HERE ARE NOW TWELVE million RVs in the hands of American families. That's a lot of happy campers. If this keeps up, eventually we'll all be living in RVs, nobody will have an address, and the post office will be stuck with all those zip codes.

What are all these RVers looking for, out there on the highways and byways? It's the freedom to go whenever they please, staying wherever they like, as long as they like. Freedom from the tyranny of alarm clocks, and the numbing routines of a workaday existence. Freedom to live a totally new and independent lifestyle that they can make up as they go along.

Many RVers are like migratory birds, flocking north in the summer and south every winter to the sunshine belt. Some, like the swallows of Capistrano, return to favorite places year after year. We met several families who drive up to Alaska's Kenai Peninsula every summer to catch and freeze a year's supply of salmon and halibut. The money they save on fish dinners helps finance their sports fishing vacations.

RV parks where travelers congregate are like instant villages, changing every day. Incoming travelers roll their awnings down, set up their lawn chairs and barbecues, and begin swapping stories of where they've been. Visiting with park neighbors is a good way to learn about new places you'd want to see yourself.

The typical RVer is a mainstream American. We met hardware executives and dentists, ex-cops and auto dealers, long-haul truckers (very handy guys to know!), teachers, artists, carpenters, and former military people who'd been all over the globe.

Equally varied were their vehicles. While most drove average priced, popular brand rigs, we also saw a number of huge, elaborately equipped RVs that looked like big cousins of stretch limos. Some of our more affluent brethren spend $500,000 and up for these bus-sized, luxury land yachts. The ultimate big spender we heard about is a classical music lover from Laguna Beach, California who never uses his half-million dollar toy except for a leisurely commute down the freeway to San Diego for the opera season.

RVing has obviously come a long way from its tent trailer origins some forty years ago. Dealers and service shops are easy to find throughout North America, along with camping facilities that run the gamut from no-frills desert "boondocking" to luxury resorts like country clubs. No wonder RVs keep growing in popularity.

An RV eliminates much of the hassle of getting from one place to another. You don't have to worry about missing a flight, getting stuck at an airport, or discovering that your luggage was shipped to Iceland or Tanganyika.

For vacationing young families, it's a chance to hang onto their sanity and their wallets at the same time. Having a home on wheels can be much easier than parading a tribe of wild progeny in and out of restaurants all day and into motels each night. While it's also true that an RV full of kids can stretch a mother's nerves until they twang like a cheap banjo, there's always the great outdoors to calm down in.

For fishermen, backpackers, trail bikers and cross-country skiers, an RV can be a great way to get up into the back country — and it serves as a cabin in the woods as well. Many wives who've gone camping in tents, cooked over wood fires and come home smelling like smoked salmon find they much prefer RV-style camping with a real stove, sink and shower, and a genuine bed besides.

Hobbyists ranging from rock and gem collectors to show dog owners depend on RVs for traveling to shows and conventions with all their gear aboard.

For older Americans yearning to travel, an RV is the ultimate dream machine. What better time than retirement to make that dream come true?

Most seniors today are still active and healthy. Not content to sit around gathering moss, many would rather be rolling down the highway in an RV, enjoying a whole new life of travel and adventure.

Fortunately for retired couples on a modest budget, RVing can stretch that travel dollar until it looks like a green string. Just eating and sleeping aboard an RV whittles costs down considerably. Many couples supplement their incomes by turning their hobbies and crafts into extra cash, or by taking part-time jobs along the way.

There's a growing trend for retirees to live in their RVs full time, according to writer Gaylord

Maxwell, who ranks as one of America's most experienced experts on RV travel. He says in his useful book *Fulltiming* that more than three quarters of a million Americans now live in their rigs.

Wife Ethel and I full-timed for eighteen months after retiring. We kept meeting happy wanderers who said they would never, never want to go back to living in one place. All seemed happily married. They'd better be, because an RV with its limited quarters is no place for a couple whose eyes glaze over at the sight of each other.

Within a month of retiring on the road, I felt so laid back that I was practically horizontal. Life was as close to being carefree as either of us had ever experienced. But we knew we'd want a home base some day, so we decided to turn our wanderings into a search for a place to retire.

If you really want to taste the flavor of a place, nothing beats arriving in an RV and lingering for a week or more, soaking up impressions of the people and how they live. You can visit all sorts of likely locales at your leisure, and then narrow your choices to suit your personal needs and preferences.

We found several places that ranked high on our list, ranging from big cities like Seattle to a tiny town on Canada's Salt Spring Island, off the coast of British Columbia. Eventually we chose to settle in Durango, Colorado, amid the soaring Rocky Mountain scenery that first drew us there as travelers. With so much to do outdoors, it's a town where it's easy to keep healthy and fit as the years go by.

(Many Rockies seniors are rock-sturdy specimens. My personal hero is a 66-year-old retired doctor with an enormous zest for life who zooms down the ski slopes like a pro, despite having two artificial hips. When he isn't skiing, he's swimming a mile at a time, and lifting weights. With friends like him, you have to stay in shape just to stay in touch.)

As much as we appreciate having roots in a great little town, Ethel and I are revving up to hit the road again. RVing is just too much fun to stay put indefinitely. Ethel, who once had to be dragged kicking and screaming into a motorhome, now enjoys the casual convenience of RV travel as much as I do.

Maybe we'll head south to see New Orleans, where the Cajuns have a saying that seems to fit RVing: "Laissez les bon temps rouler" . . . let the good times roll!

How to publish your story and win a book

Do you have a funny story about traveling in an RV? Send it to Ray Parker for his forthcoming sequel to "RV Having Fun Yet?"

If your story is selected, you'll receive an autographed copy of the new book, tentatively titled "RV Tales." Upon publication, you will also be given credit in print as author of the story, unless you wish to remain anonymous.

Ray is looking for a variety of actual RV experiences— the funniest, most unforgettable, most embarrassing, the best, the worst, etc. that have ever happened to you or other RVers that you've heard about. Submit as many stories as you like. All those accepted will be edited for publication.

Please type or print your story. Send it to:

Ray Parker
c/o Oldfield Publishing
PO Box 1387
Durango, CO 81302

If yours is selected, you will be notified by mail in advance of publication.

"RV Having Fun Yet?" — A Great Gift

Wondering what to get that RVer in your family for Father's Day or Christmas, or that birthday coming up? He'll enjoy having a copy of *RV Having Fun Yet?*

It's also a fun book for travel lovers as well as folks nearing retirement who've been dreaming of having an RV themselves some day.

Send completed order form to:

Oldfield Publishing
PO Box 1387
Durango, CO 81302

ORDER FORM

Send ____ copies of *RV Having Fun Yet?* at $12.95, plus $3 shipping and handling per book. (Colorado residents please include $.91 sales tax.) Canadian orders require a postal money order in US. funds. Allow four weeks for delivery.

☐ Check/Money Order for $_____ enclosed
☐ Charge my ☐ Visa ☐ MC

Card #_____ Expires_____

Signature _____

Name _____

Company_____

Address _____

City/State/Zip _____

Phone (_____)_____

About the Author

Ray Parker is a veteran TV comedy writer, lecturer and magazine humor columnist who traveled the country with his wife Ethel in an RV after retiring from a successful career in Hollywood.

He has written material for numerous celebrities, including Art Linkletter, Bob Hope, Dinah Shore and Dick Van Dyke. While on Hope's staff for three years, he wrote monologue material for the Bob Hope TV Specials, the Academy Awards, and Hope's numerous live appearances through the world.

Ray began his television career as head writer for "Art Linkletter's House Party," the top-rated daytime show on CBS-TV. While with Linkletter and producer John Guedel, he also wrote the CBS Radio show, "Dear Abby" for advice columnist Abigail Van Buren.

After writing on staff for Dinah Shore, Ray was hired by game show creator Mark Goodson as a writer-producer for GoodsonTodman. He then signed with Joe Barbera of Hanna-Barbera Productions, becoming a senior writing executive for several animation series, including new episodes of "The Flintstones."

Ray went on to become production executive in charge of writers for 65 live half-hour episodes of the award-winning children's television series, "Zoobilee Zoo." This popular series, created by Hallmark Properties and produced by DIC Productions, began as a syndicated commercial show. It was soon picked up for numerous reruns by major PBS stations for its entertaining approach to children's imaginations and creativity.